THE ROSES AND THE THORNS IN THE CAREER OF AN INFORMATION SCIENTIST

A Managerial Insight

THE ROSES AND THE THORNS IN THE CAREER OF AN INFORMATION SCIENTIST
A Managerial Insight

G. J. NARAYANA

Ess Ess Publications
New Delhi

THE ROSES AND THE THORNS
IN THE CAREER OF AN INFORMATION SCIENTIST
A Managerial Insight

ISBN: 978-81-934311-4-6

First Published 2018

Published by:
Ess Ess Publications
4831/24, Ansari Road,
Darya Ganj,
New Delhi-110 002.
INDIA
Phones: 23260807, 41563444
Fax: 41563334
E-mail: info@essessreference.com
www.essessreference.com

Cover Design by *Patch Creative Unit*

Printed at
Yash Printographics, Noida

Acknowledgments

My sincere thanks to Prof. M. R. Riswadkar, former Professor in the Department of Library and Information Science, University of Poona, Puna. Shri H.G. Desai, former Chief Librarian, Institute of Armamemt Technology (now DIAT), Pune for their evaluation and valuable suggestions; Mrs. Jayashri Kanitkar and Mrs. Seema Tare, Scientists, Armamemt Research and Development Establishment, Pune for going through the draft manuscript and editorial help; Shri M.N. Nadgir, my grand children Shri P.N. Pranav Rao and Dr. P.N. Kasturi Rao for their help in computer work; my wife Smt. G.N. Vedavathi for her active cooperation; Shri Y. J. Raghunatha Reddy, Chartered Accountant, Bengaluru, Shri Chikkamallaiah, the former Librarian, IIM, Bengaluru and my friend Shri. H. Achhutha for their encouragement.

Contents

Preface

Life is a collection of experiences lived through, coupled with learning. The dictionary meanings of the term 'experience' include "wisdom derived from the changes and trials of life; the passing through of any event or course of events by which one is affected". Learning is what one acquires in the form of information/ knowledge/skill. Experience and knowledge held by individuals vary from person to person. They are largely the products of one's chosen field of activity or profession or career. It is also the summation of the feelings or knowledge representing the results of action and reaction of persons to a given situation or encounter. Experiences of people range from commonplace to unique or extraordinary. There is no definite yardstick to indicate whether the experiences are commonplace or unique. Yet, it is possible to differentiate between what is unique and what is ordinary, though such characterization is subjective. When the experiences narrated are unique, they are likely to be of interest to others. They convey the wisdom or lack of it shown by the parties involved in the experiences culled out from the situation or incident. They may also serve as frameworks for comparison helping others to learn from those experiences by understanding, analyzing and drawing inferences from them, and taking them into consideration while formulating responses to similar situations. It is necessary to bear in mind that the experience of one person and his or her response to a situation need not be the same as the experiences of other persons faced with similar situation. This is primarily due to the fact that one's action or response to an action is shaped by one's personality, previous experiences, traits of character, and value system, which differ from person to person, and the work culture of the organization. Hence, in judging a given experience as good or bad, right or wrong there could always be a different or even opposite version of the same experience when seen from the angle of the other party involved in the incident or situation. Experience serves two purposes: - a) It is a source of information/ knowledge, and b) also a means of learning. Rich sources of recorded experiences pertaining to social living are proverbs, biographies and autobiographies.

The account of the experiences, and the thoughts and reflections narrated here is drawn from the working life of the author in the domain of library and information service, and teaching of management science in different managerial capacities, over a period of three decades beginning from 1955. The institutions served include the central government secretariat, a large private industry, national science documentation centre, a publications unit, a higher institute of technology and a large defence R&D establishment. Except for the experience in industry, all other incidents narrated here are from working in the government and semi-government sector. These experiences would have taken a different turn had the field of action been that of private sector. However, irrespective of the action domain and the field of work the basic managerial principles remain the same. The main difference between the experiences encountered in the two sectors relates to organization's motive and structure, relative freedom to act, accountability, job security, customer relationships, policies and rules governing the enterprise. Every move in the private industry is dictated primarily or solely by profit motive, which is not so in the functioning of governments; the former is managed, and the latter is administered. These differences have definite bearings on the nature of experience that follows in working in the two fields.

Since these experiences are intertwined with individuals involved in the given situation or incident, it becomes unavoidable to give the names of the persons tied with the particular experience or encounter. In certain instances, to avoid unpleasantness and maintain dignity, the names of such persons are changed and indicated so. There is no intention whatsoever, on the part of the author to denigrate the concerned individual/s or organizations, but to give the true picture. As the accounts of the experiences are drawn from the author's memory and records, it is possible that a few minor discrepancies could have entered the narration, but they do not affect the validity of contents and contentions of the experiences in a major way.

The topics in the text are arranged in the order of: 1. Developing positive work culture; 2. Recruitment, performance review; 3. Projects, operations and accountability; 4. Authority and its exercise; 5.Libraries and book-sellers, E-publications; 6. Discipline; 7. Quality maintenance, Brand building; 8. Educational functions of libraries; 9. Language skill; 10. Career: Updating of knowledge/skills; 11. Recognizing and rewarding merit; 12. Mentors, Inspiring leaders; and 13. Fulfilment. At the end of each of these topic the relevant thought/principle underlying the text is examined, interpreted and its essence is presented as analysis.

The experiences and thoughts on various topics narrated here may also be seen as case studies for persons studying organizational/personnel management. Since these experiences are scanned from the era of mid-twentieth century, a major limitation is that the impact of the following factors is missed out: Internet revolution, telecommunication technology and mobile telephony and their corresponding influences on individuals' aspirations and attitudes, his or her basic values, and selection of role models, which in turn give a new twist to the living in the information society or knowledge society. As a consequence, the earlier time and space-gap that existed in society have been literally bridged. This has added a new dimension to the affairs of humans and the resulting experiences. At the same time it has led to a new divide in society, between a new generation which is technology savvy, impatient and highly money-oriented, and the old generation still holding on to old ways of living.

The effects of the thoughts, views and experiences narrated here, as far as the individual reader is concerned, could be positive, negative or even of no consequence. The sweet experiences leading to inner satisfaction, feeling of achievement or even pride are like roses. Bad experiences, like thorns, are prickly and are likely to lead to dissatisfaction, frustration, a sense being wronged and even hatred towards the perceived perpetrators of that bad experience. This text is a collection of such thorns and roses.

G.J. Narayana

1

Developing Positive Work Culture

All social organizations are built on the principle of cooperation: cooperation between the members constituting the group, and between the groups and other stakeholders. This concept of cooperation viewed in the context of an organization as a whole constitutes a general principle. In practice, cooperation operates at the level of smaller groups of persons organized into divisions, departments and sections that make up the whole organization. The term 'team' is generally used for a group of persons specially constituted to carryout a specific project or activity with a set time limit. Team building and promoting team spirit (at the general as well as specific level) to a large extent depends on the team leader. A successful team leader has to have many special abilities. A few of such attributes are highlighted here through case studies, from which we can derive a few axioms on getting the best from the staff.

1. ASSIGN A JOB TO MATCH THE ABILITIES OF THE INDIVIDUAL

Mrs. Sarla Singh (name changed) was a middle aged officer working in the library[1] of the Aeronautical Development Establishment (ADE)[2], Bangalore with nothing much to look forward to in her remaining years of service. Before my joining

ADE she was a sidelined person. Given her limitations of technical abilities and drive, it seems, the senior authorities above her were neither able to create self confidence in her nor get the best out of her abilities. On her part, she was reconciled to the situation. The problem before me was to find out for her the most suitable area of work, where she could excel. Managing a large library involves a lot of liaison work with other units of the establishment, like Director's secretariat, research divisions, workshop, stores section, accounts department, administration, and transportation section and outside agencies. This is an important but thankless job. Not everybody can fill this position successfully. The person entrusted with this type of assignment needs to have special personal skills to liaison, and the temperament to enjoy the work. A careful assessment of her abilities and temperament showed that she was endowed with two excellent traits, namely skill of persuasion and patience. Hence, the liaison work was entrusted to her as her primary responsibility besides some routine work. It was an excellent decision, and she proved her excellence in her new position. There are several instances in my experiences where this principle has worked very successfully.

Managerial insight : Nature does not create all human beings with the same level of intelligence, skill, drive and aptitude. In general, it is found that every individual is gifted with some special skill and aptitude in consonance with the left brain- right brain phenomenon. It is for the manager to identify those traits and make use of them to the best advantage of the organization, and the concerned individual. The managerial ability lies in assigning a job that can exploit fully the skills and aptitude of the employee- axiom number 1.

2. DEVELOP THE ATTITUDE OF EMPATHY

The interest of employees in an organization may be classified into: a) career connected and b) emotional and humanism related. The career aspect is mainly concerned with selection, performance assessment, promotion, knowledge update and skill development, and recognition and reward—the functions of Human Resource Management (HRM). Though employment is treated strictly as a contract between the employer and the employee, the emotional and human aspects of employees cannot be ignored. Given here is a case relating to human aspect of management.

(a) The Case of Maternity Leave : Mrs. Mary Phillips (name changed) was working as Secretarial Assistant in the ADE library. By temperament she was a cheerful lady endowed with understanding nature. She knew her job well and always displayed a high sense of responsibility. In a way, she represented the collective conscience of the lady co-workers in the library. She sorted out many of their relational problems in the office, thus helping me in management. Of late she seemed always worried and something was eating her up. This affected her work. For the first time, she started staying absent from work. She would not tell me what was going wrong with her.

One morning, she sent through her husband a leave note accompanied by a medical certificate. She wanted 60 days extraordinary medical/maternity leave with full salary. The doctor had certified that she had an abortion and had advised her two months bed rest. I could not believe it. I wanted to know the true facts. Before I could speak further, her husband desired to speak to me in confidence. He confided in me that Mrs. Mary had asked him to state the truth behind her request for medical leave. The fact was that she had exhausted all her normal leave due to her, and if the extraordinary leave was not sanctioned, she would be deprived of her monthly salary. Presently, they were passing through serious personal and family problems, and also a severe financial crisis. Without salary she and her family were in the danger of ruin. He also narrated the nature and extent of their problems, and their critical financial position. Further, he added that he was speaking the truth and leaving the decision to me.

The situation posed a moral dilemma to me. By sanctioning the leave she and her family would be saved from the hopeless situation, but on my part I would be a party to the deception. On the other hand, if I refused leave I would be on the right side of rules, but there was the possibility of the future of a whole family being jeopardized. Further, stating the reasons for refusing leave would possibly attract disciplinary action against her. Then I remembered Air Cdr. S.K Nair's action in the case of Mr. Kapale (see 6.1), which guided me in arriving at the decision of granting the leave she had asked for. Granting leave turned out to be the right decision. She regained her confidence, overcame her problems and came back to her original state of mind.

(b) The Problem of Social Predicament : Mrs. Archanadevi (name changed) was appointed as an attendant under the central government policy of giving employment to one member of the family of the employee in the event of his or her death while still in service. She was posted to ADE knowledge centre. One of the main functions of the attendant was collection of letters and parcels meant for the library from the Central Receipt and Dispatch Section and outward delivery of letters from the library to different departments and sections. Mrs. Archanadevis' deceased husband was holding the position of a designer and was respected. After working for two days on the assigned job she came to me, in a highly disturbed mood with tears in her eyes, and requested for a change of assignment. She also said that she is willing to do any work other than courier type that she may be assigned. Her reason for asking for change of duty was that given her social background and the fact that her husband was holding a designer's post and his death is still fresh in the minds of people in the establishment she is finding it quite embarrassing to show her face as a mail carrying attendant. Since it was a genuine predicament not of her making, but forced by circumstances, her work assignment was changed to that of stack maintenance and assisting readers in locating publications. This action created heartburn in the other attendant working in the unit whose assignment also included carrying dak. He came to me and complained that I was partial to Mrs. Archanadevi. When I explained to him the reason for my action and requested him to put himself in his colleague's position and think. It was his goodness that he accepted my reasons behind my action and was with me in expressing his sympathy for the lady.

Managerial insight : Was my decision right in the case of Mrs. Phillips? Viewed from the surface level, it was not a right course; but it certainly was a wise decision. It was justified because the positive effects of granting the leave far outweighed the net adverse effects that would have resulted from rejecting the leave. Sanctioning of leave did flout the rules (at least on paper) and resulted in minor loss to the government. The vital consideration in favour of the lady was her value to the organization and her truthfulness. It resulted in making her more loyal to the organization with an enhanced stake in the well-being of the organization. However, one could still view the situation differently. In the case of Mrs. Archanadevi, the problem was about convincing the other attendant on the justness of the decision. In most cases convincing in a manner that the discontented party understands the reasons behind your stand rather than exercising authority yields better results. Taking an empathetic attitude towards coworkers, barring exceptions, make them reciprocate with show of greater sense of responsibility in their work and increased loyalty to the organization- axiom number 2.

3. EFFECTIVE COMMUNICATIONS IS BASIC TO TEAM-BUILD UP

It has been my routine practice to go round each section, talk to the persons there and satisfy myself that things are moving smoothly. This practice reduced the barrier between me and my coworkers irrespective of their ranks. It also helped raise the level of confidence among colleagues and created mutual respect for each other. The essence of this measure is enhancing rapport and encouraging dialogue between the higher executives and co-workers/subordinates and overcoming the inherent weakness found in a hierarchical structure. I recapitulated this practice, some twenty years later, when one of my former colleagues focused on this aspect and its positive impact on the staff while our discussion shifted to the changes in the pattern of management of Knowledge Centre (KC) of ADE, then and now. What prompted me to follow this practice was the annual inspection conducted by one of the Deans at the Institute of Armament Technology (IAT), Pune. On the inspection day, the Dean accompanied by the Chief Administrative Officer (CAO) and the General Staff Officer (GSO) went round all the major service departments of the Institute to get a firsthand feel of their functioning. This also helped the units maintain inspection standards, at least for that period; and create a feeling among the employees that the Head of the Institution cares for their Unit. IAT being a large organization with a number of functional units, even keeping one day aside in a year for inspection of each major section would have been not easy. The KC of ADE being a small unit employing about 20 persons (+ 20 workers of the Reprographic section when it was under my charge), following this practice was not difficult, but rewarding.

Managerial insight : The practice of taking a round of each unit at regular intervals and talking to the persons working in various sections with an open mind will help enhance effective communication in the unit. This, in turn helps the manager exercise proper control. For the staff members it gives the opportunity to share their problems, if any, and find collective solutions to the problems. It also enhances mutual regard for one another overcoming the barrier of status. The objective of the visit should be to understand and help co-workers and not to find fault or keep a watch on them due to lack of trust in them. Such visits should not turn out into unwarranted interference in their work. Maintaining healthy communication and interaction with employees through means such as taking rounds of each section and meetings helps understand their problems, if any, build good rapport with them, share responsibility, and improve the functioning of the unit as a whole- axiom number 3.

4. ALLOWING DOMAIN FREEDOM HELPS TO GET THE BEST OUT OF A WORKER

Prof. M.R. Riswadkar, the newly appointed Reader in the Department of Library and Information Science, University of Poona telephoned to me that he wanted to discuss with me on a matter relating to the M. Lib. Sc. Course, which was to commence from August 1979. I did not know him personally till then. I had only seen the project report submitted by him for his M. Lib. Sc. degree of Bombay University to ascertain the pattern of writing the report, which I had greatly admired, when I registered for the same course many years later. Over tea in a restaurant he told me that the University was starting the M.Lib.Sc.course. He wanted the students to be exposed to the modern concepts of management, its techniques and methods, and its application to libraries. This would form one of the four papers constituting the Course, namely *Management of Libraries and Information Centres*. He had been on the lookout for a suitable teacher who could take up the assignment. He told me that Prof. B. Anderson (teacher to both of us at Bombay University) had suggested my name. He also showed me the portion of the syllabus relating to management of libraries. I was not at all happy with the syllabus. There was nothing in the syllabus about management. It only covered the traditional aspects of library administration. I expressed my readiness to teach provided I was given the freedom to choose the timing and the duration of each lecture as I was engaged between 0730 hrs to 1330hours at IAT, the freedom to select the topics to be covered, and the level of treatment of the topics. Given the rules and regulations of the University, it was not easy for him to agree to my conditions. It is to his credit that he agreed to my request. I was giving 15 to 20 lectures on the subject of management every year. I taught the subject for fifteen years, as a guest lecturer, beginning in1979 to 1994 and for another two years after my shifting to ADE, Bangalore. During those seventeen years, Prof. Riswadkar never asked me even once what I was teaching, and how I was teaching. It is one of the very rare privileges that a teacher can hope for. It is this freedom and the confidence that Prof. Anderson and Prof. Riswadkar had in me and in my ability to do justice to the the subject, as well as to the students that bound me all those years to give my best to the course. One example of the freedom given to me as a teacher and how it motivated me to give my best to the students is given below.

Demonstration through Practice : 'Role playing' is one of the techniques in management training and formulating development programmes. The technique consists of selecting real–life situations, simulating the same by assigning roles to the interacting parties and studying how they behave as original characters and react as assumed individuals in the created situation and drawing useful inferences. A role is a comprehensive pattern of behaviour associated with the position[3]. Role play provides a simulated reality experience of the problem or situation as reflected by the role players' behavioural responses, which are unpredictable and vary. Hence, role play can be used as a valuable training aid.

A lecture on role play[3] was one of the items I was covering under the topic Creativity/Organization development. Lectures can only describe and explain what role play is, how it is to be conducted and what are its uses. No lectures on role play can ever give the actual feeling and the experience of acting the role to the students. This is because there is a wide gap between what we teach and lecture and its actualization and experiencing. Actual participation gives the participants live experience with all the various features and nuances, actions and emotions played by the roles. The behaviour of each role will be on display and thereby one can observe, analyze the situation, evaluate the action of each participant in relation to the problem, and draw proper conclusions to arrive at the solutions to a problem. Realizing this, I decided to supplement the lecture by actually conducting a role play.

The topic for the role play was chosen from the area of reference service related to a real problem. The roles were that of the reference librarian and a set of users with their problems. Each role was assigned to a student. The session was open to the students of M.Lib and B.Lib courses, teachers, and staff members of the University library. I was surprised at the enthusiasm shown by the participants. The freedom given to me in teaching prompted me to try this novel way of connecting the lecture with practice.

It is on the foundation of these lectures, many years later, that my book on library and information management came to be written[3]. A few years later, when we were reminiscing about the Course, Prof. Riswadkar told me that when he disclosed at a conference of librarians and information scientists how the management topic was introduced to the students of M.Lib.Sc., and how he had kept track of my lectures, many in the audience were amazed. He had requested one of the bright students in the class to keep a module-wise note of the topics of all my lectures and their coverage. For the subsequent years these topics formed the syllabus of the course.

Managerial insight : When a work is entrusted to a person or a team, noninterference and giving freedom to the assignee or the team leader to design, programme and execute the work gets the best out of the assignee- axiom no.4. Before entrusting the task it is essential for the manager to make sure that the selected person or the team leader has the requisite knowledge, ability and involvement. The common practice followed while assigning a task is to explain what is to be done and how it is to be done. Invariably, the 'Why' aspect of the job is missed. Explaining the importance of the task and indicating the context enables the worker to exercise her or his thinking power and bring in a creative ability to the work. 'Role play' is a management training programme that can be usefully employed to understand a given real situation or problem through simulated experience.

5. BE IN THE DRIVER'S SEAT

I have been fortunate to be in the driver's seat all through my professional career (barring the three years I spent in the industry), holding independent charge as head of a section (Central Secretariat Library, New Delhi), project head (INSDOC, New Delhi), head of Documentation Unit (Publications and Information Directorate, CSIR, New Delhi); Head of Library and Information Centre, IAT, Pune and Scientist-E heading ADE Knowledge Centre. To be in the driver's seat means having the authority to control vested in the position. Generally, it takes ten to fifteen years of working experience and exposure to get into the driver's seat, which has not been so in my case. To be in the driver's seat is a privilege, because it gives freedom to shape the destiny of the unit in the way one wants, convert dreams into reality; and to put one's creative thoughts and plans into action. It is also a responsibility because one is answerable for the outcome of one's actions and lack of actions. The main reason for whatever I have been able to accomplish is the privilege of independence to act that came my way. Of course, the independence to act has to be within the rules and broad policies governing the parent organization of which the library is a part.

Managerial insight : To hold independent charge of a unit is a responsibility and a privilege. How one makes use of this privilege to the best interest of the users and the organization, and discharges the responsibilities of the position determine one's success or failure. It is a privilege as it opens the vista of opportunities to put into action one's talent and abilities, and a responsibility because one is answerable for the consequences of the initiatives taken. Roses as well as thorns are yours, and there is no one to pass on the buck to in case of failure. Not all persons want to be in the driver's seat, unless he or she has the requisite temperament, drive and desire. Without being in the driver's seat, one will not be able to achieve anything substantial and noteworthy.

REFERENCES AND NOTES

1. Renamed Information Centre and Library (IC&L), and later Knowledge Centre (KC).
2. A unit of Defence Research and Development Establishment (DRDO), Bangalore, Government of India
3. Narayana, G.J. Library and Information Management. New Delhi, Prentice-Hall of India, 1991.

2

Recruitment : Performance Review

Organizations to function need people. The number, the type and the caliber of the required people and their relative positions in the organization are decided by the organization structure. Once these are established, the process of recruitment/ placement begins. Selection and placement of persons is dictated by the tasks and functions assigned to the position, the nature of work, type of responsibilities and the requisite authority needed to get the task or function performed to the set standards. Hence, assessment of performance of existing staff members on a continuous basis and in the case of fresh recruitment assessment of the job seeker's ability and suitability to perform the functions assigned to the position constitutes a key parameter in the selection process. The Human Resources Development (HRD) department exists for planning, staffing, organizing and developing the requisite manpower for the proper functioning of the organization.

In selecting candidates for junior positions requiring specialized skills, it is advisable to test their skills besides the interview performance. For senior positions it is the candidate's performance in the interview, experience in the field, managerial ability, and fitness for the job that form the assessment criteria. An interview, also called personality test, is to assess objectively the depth of knowledge, capacity to understand and other intellectual traits and skills of the candidate required to suit the position. As an interview generally lasts for 30 minutes to an hour, how that time is utilized by the candidate to express clearly and cogently his/her knowledge, perception and judgment on the issues raised by the experts, is of utmost importance. A good interview takes the mode of discussion, not mere touting of information or futile argument, once the potentiality of the candidate to fill the post passes the initial test of general suitability in the minds of selectors. For interviewers, it is an arduous task, and they must ensure that justice is done to all the candidates. The first step in the interview process is to make the candidate feel at home. Questions asked should be fair, objective and relevant to the job. The philosophy should be to see that the best candidate who fits the requirements of the position is selected. The interviewer's personal bias should be kept aside. A candidate must be assessed for actual competency as well as his or her potential to develop and deliver. When there are departmental candidates (persons already serving in the organization), fairness demands that the insider is preferred over the external candidate, provided the difference in their overall performance is very marginal.

In an interview the behaviour displayed by the candidate plays a significant role. The interviewers, by and large, form their first general impression about the candidate by observing his or her behaviour. Important factors that makeup one's behaviour are physical appearance including dress, and body language. The body language reflects to a certain extent the person's psychological makeup, such as self confidence, anxiety, diffidence, temperament and habits. However, central to the interview in the minds of the interviewer are the job related themes such as knowledge and skill, experience, grasping capacity, convictions and value system of the candidate.

Before coming for the interview, the candidate must prepare well. It is essential for the candidate to know as much as possible about the organization and the position to which she or he is taking the interview. The candidate must be candid in answering questions. The interviewers on the board should be wise enough to see through false pretences put-up by a candidate. Some times, a self-conducted SWOT (Strength-Weakness- Opportunity- Threats) analysis vis-à-vis the requirements of the job, prepares the candidate well in facing the interview (Srinivasan, 2014). If the candidate is not sure about his or her fitness for the job, there is no point in taking the interview. Some of my experiences as an interviewee and also as an interviewer are narrated here.

Locating Candidates for Recruitment. Any action of actual selection of personnel begins with identifying the source/pool of candidates available for appointment. Main avenues used for locating candidates available for recruitment are- a) approaching employment exchanges in the case of recruitment by government agencies, b) advertising in newspapers/ online channels, c) employing private manpower search/HRD agencies and c) make use of employee referral programs. Employee referral programs are prevalent mostly in industry which is discussed here, as the features of other channels are generally known.

1. CANDIDATES SPONSORED BY EMPLOYMENT EXCHANGE

For me, like many others coming from Southern India, Delhi was the 'rising sun' city for central government employment in the 1950s. I was selected for the post of Librarian Grade-III in the Ministry of Defence library. But receiving the appointment letter was long delayed due to time taken for completion of police verification and other formalities. Hence, I needed a job immediately. I had registered my name in the Delhi Employment Exchange (DEE), but with no positive results. I approached Mr.N.M. Ketkar, the Chief Librarian of the Central Secretariat Library (CSL), Government of India with whom I was briefly acquainted when he was the Deputy Librarian at the Benaras Hindu University, and expressed my difficulties of living in Delhi without a job. He informed me about the existing vacancy in his library, and asked me to apply for it. With this information, I approached the DEE and requested them to sponsor my name. They informed me that there was no such vacancy. When I conveyed this information to Mr. Ketkar, he was kind enough to give me the reference details of the letter sent to DEE intimating the vacancy. Armed with the reference details, I again went to DEE and requested them to forward my name. This time they had no other option but to sponsor my name. After an interview, I was selected for the post and I joined the CSL, my first entry into the library and information profession. The account of this interview is narrated later (see 9.1).

It turned out that the DEE authorities had withheld from sponsoring my name as I had a postgraduate diploma in library science, whereas all the other competitors had only a certificate in library science, besides a degree. Sponsoring my name would have reduced the chances of other candidates competing for selection. It seems that the certificate holders had managed to influence the DEE authorities to withhold my candidature or the DEE authorities were expecting commission/ bribe money from me.

Managerial insight : The malpractices - in recruitment and promotion, we hear of today in the government employment area both at the centre and the states, were there even in the early days of independent India, though not in the same scale or form. Things seems to have improved a little with the creation of institutions like *Lokayukta.*

2. EMPLOYEE REFERRAL PROGRAM

As the name indicates, it is a method wherein the employees already working in a given organization are encouraged by the management to recommend persons they know for employment at suitable positions in the organization. For this the employee is suitably rewarded. The advantages of this system are that it saves the management substantial amounts of time and energy involved in the search for talented persons required to fill up positions in the given organization. Votaries of referral program claim that it enriches organizational culture and forms a ready source of identifying new talent as the referee happens to be an employee. Being a serving employee, he or she will be well aware of the needs of the job and about the referred person in terms of requisite skills, ability and other characteristics. Its detractors note that employee referral program leads to favoritism/nepotism, promotes mediocrity and inhibits creative thinking in the enterprise

(Sharma, 2016). Indian companies adopting referral programme include Infosys, Tata Chemicals and NIIT Technologies.

3. THROUGH ADVERTISEMENT IN MEDIA

A major avenue of locating candidates for recruitment by organizations is through open advertisement in news papers and other media channels including social networks.

Importance of Proper Drafting of Advertisement : It is important to ensure that the advertisement is clearly drafted showing what is required in the employee in terms of age, qualifications, experience and other specifics. Relaxations in the stipulated conditions, if any, the advertisement must clearly indicate them, and must be scrupulously adhered to while selecting. The following case of advertisement for the selection of Chief Librarian shows the unfairness resulting from not adhering to this principle:

One of the prestigious educational and research institute in Bangalore had advertized for the post of Chief librarian. I had applied for the post. There was an age limit prescribed for the position. But the advertisement had clearly stated that *the age limit is relaxable for otherwise deserving cases.* I was over aged by three years. Before sending my application, I had specifically confirmed from the concerned authorities of the Institute that I was eligible for applying to the post though I was over aged. I was called for the interview presided over by the Director of the Institute, a scholar of international repute. My interview began and ended with just one sentence coming from the Chairman of the Interview Committee. He stated that since I was over aged, my candidature couldn't be considered. Without citing the age relaxation clause mentioned in the advertisement, I walked out of the venue in deference to the high regard I have for the institution. What hurt me most was not that I was not considered for the post, but the manner of terminating my interview. Why should the institute waste my time as well as that of the elite members of the Selection Committee by calling me to attend the interview when they had already decided not to relax the age requirement? Still, there was a silver lining to this episode, which was that the Chairman of the Committee displayed his forthrightness of character by not playing a game with me by conducting a sham interview to reject my candidature.

Managerial insight : While framing the advertisements for posts, it is essential to clearly specify the requirements of the post, the requisite qualifications, experience, age limit and other requisite elements. It is incumbent on the selectors to strictly adhere to the terms indicated in the advertisement. Failing to adhere to these terms will harm the interests of the organization and affect its reputation.

4. ACADEMIC RECORD VS. PROFESSIONAL ACHIEVEMENT

The Selection Committee chaired by a UPSC member met in IAT, Poona (now Pune) to interview candidates from the DRDO establishments in Poona for promotion from Scientist D to E. I was one of the candidates. When VIPs and VVIPs visited IAT, a visit to Information Centre & Library (IC&L) invariably used to be a part of the visitors' agenda. The day before the interview, the Chairman of the Selection Committee had visited the IC&L and had seen the services we were rendering. The interview went well. At the end of the interview, the Chairman asked me whether he could ask a personal question. I answered that he could ask, without any hesitation, any question he liked. He asked me that considering my remarkable achievement in my field, how that my educational record up to the degree level was quite ordinary. I had passed my Pre-university course and the Bachelor of Science degree examinations in third class. Truthfully, I replied that by nature, my mental makeup was philosophical, and at that period of time I was wondering what was the use of all these degrees.... Before I could proceed further, he stopped me, thanked me, and said he could understand. I was selected for promotion; and, I learnt, that my name was at the top of the list. Later, I came to know that at the party given in his honour at ARDE, the Chairman openly expressed his appreciation of the work done by IAT library, and extolled what dedication and involvement could achieve. This, I was told, created a mild stir among the scientists who had gathered there.

Managerial insight : It is not always true that the highest academic record ensures outstanding achievements. There are other factors, such as creative work environment, a passion to achieve, willingness to accept challenges, right mentorship, genuine appreciation, sufficient freedom to work which are also required to make an outstanding achiever.

5. REFERENCES AND REFEREEING

In a selection process, whether it is for employment or awarding a scholarship or admission to an educational institute the report rendered by the referees, named by the applicant, on the suitability and other relevant factors about the applicant serve as an important criterion to the selectors in arriving at the selection decision. A reference is a testimonial given by a person well acquainted with the applicant either as employer/boss or teacher or mentor, on the abilities, character and fitness of the applicant for the position or opportunity he or she is seeking. Referencing constitutes checking the background of the applicant.

Reports given by referees, I am sure, have contributed significantly in my professional success. The recommendation letter given by Dr. S.R.Ranganathan is one of the factors that enabled me to get admission as well as a studentship in a prestigious American university. Similarly, I believe that the testimonials given by Mr. B.S. Kesavan (Padma Shri), Prof. S. Parthasarathy, and Prof. B.Anderson have definitely played a part in the award of Fulbright fellowship to me. The effectiveness of the references depends, to a great extent, on the professional standing of the referee. The relationship between the applicant candidate and the referee is unique in some respects. A rare shocking instance, which is in my personal knowledge, is the one where the applicant drafted the contents of the recommendation and sent it to the referee requesting him to sign the reference letter. The referee- a deep scholar, great teacher and an esteemed librarian- was greatly hurt by this behaviour of the applicant. I was also faced with a similar situation when a person, who had worked with me earlier and whose conduct and performance was most unsatisfactory came to me after my retirement requesting for a good reference (see 6.7b). The advent of Internet and social networks has provided a new dynamic means of locating candidates and ascertaining their background.

Managerial insight : References help significantly in assessing the suitability of a candidate applying for a position or seeking an opportunity. A referee is one who is intimately aware of the candidate's character, abilities, and fitness for the position he or she is applying. A referee could be a mentor or the manager under whom the applicant is working/ had worked or a teacher. It is desirable for the applicant to inform in advance the person that he or she is giving as a referee. There are firms and agencies like LinkedIn which provide reference checks for corporate employers (Zimmerman, 2013). It helps youngsters in their careers to find suitable referees/mentors and further that relationship. For mentors it gives satisfaction that their wisdom and their knowledge about the person under reference finds right application, apart from helping the assessors in their task of making right selection.

6. MODE OF ASSESSMENT: SELECTING AN EDITORIAL ASSISTANT

The Defence Science Documentation Centre (DESIDOC), New Delhi was to fill a vacancy of an Editorial Assistant through interview. I was one of the members of the Selection Committee. Selecting the candidate solely on the basis of an interview, without considering the actual writing/journalistic abilities of the candidates surprised me a little. Since the post required writing and editing skills, I felt that it would be appropriate to test the candidates also for their journalistic competence. Therefore I suggested to the Chairman that it would be appropriate to give the candidates writing and editing test. The suggestion was unanimously accepted and followed. All the candidates took the test without making it an issue. The selection was made on the basis of the candidate's editing skill and the interview performance.

Managerial insight : For positions requiring job related skills, it is advantageous to the organization to assess the candidate's skill through practical tests, in addition to his or her interview performance.

7. PERFORMANCE REVIEW

Annual review of performance of employees at all levels in an organization is the most important means of tracking and evaluating the performance over the year of each employee. Such an appraisal serves three main purposes- to establish accountability of each member in terms of overall task accomplishment during the year; to serve as a guide in evolving the requisite incentive packages for good performance; and to provide a base to initiate corrective measures in cases of under performance of employees. In other words, such reviews help in evolving the requisite incentive system to reward good performance and in developing corrective measures needed to overcome under performance of employees, which are essential for effective and efficient functioning of organizations. While rewards may take the form of granting promotion, award of bonus, citation of achievement; punishment may take the opposite form of rewards. Performance review in someway plays a part in attracting new talent to the organization and in reducing the rate of attrition. Whichever be the review system one chooses, it must result in clear, transparent and impartial appraisal.

Though industry, both in India and abroad, has employed to varying degrees of success/failure alternative performance evaluation systems, like the bell curve method (Pradeesh, 2016). Government and semi-government organizations in India, including libraries follow the traditional annual appraisal method. This has deprived government organizations becoming innovative and experimental in the adoption of new systems of performance appraisal.

Continuous Assessment of Performance : Replacement of the annual performance review of employees by the system of continuous assessment is the recent trend found across the world, particularly in the West. This takes the form of frequent check-ins between managers and employees. The continuous review overcomes the biggest drawback of the annual review, i.e., holding employees accountable for past behaviour at the expense of improving current performance and grooming talent for the future. The annual assessment was primarily meant for deciding monetary reward, where as the continuous assessment is aimed at understanding the organization's culture and goals, motivating employees to imbibe the spirit of cooperation and wholehearted involvement needed on their part to help achive the aims and objectives of the organization. Continuous assessment introduces openness, relies on getting feedback and suggestions from the employees, which the manager utilizes to improve current performance and meet the future requirements by introducing the requisite coaching, mentoring and providing developmental opportunities to employees as a continuous ongoing process. It overcomes time, space and opportunity restrictions inherent in the annual assessment and thereby act as a motivator to the employees; and make them realize their responsibilities and importance on a continuous basis. It overcomes the rigidity associated with annual review, imparts alertness among the staff members. For the organization it serves as a continuous process needed to develop its human capital through openness, collaboration and innovation to meet its current and future needs (Cappelli and Tavis). The feedback, both online and offline culled from continuous reviews helps plan suitable employee development programs. It is also in line with the expectations of the millennial workforce. Continuous appraisal is catching up in India too with leading companies like the Tata Consultancy services employing continuous assessment in place of annual and bell curve based assessment. (tcs....Google search).

(a) Criteria for Grading 'Outstanding' Performance : The following account was narrated to me by the PA to Cmde. S.S.Venakteshwaran, the then Director and Dean of IAT, Pune. The incident is related to the Director facing a tricky situation in the then concluded meeting of the Departmental Promotion Committee on account of my 'confidential report' writing on the performance of those working with me in the library. I had rated the performance of an assistant as 'outstanding'. This was the second 'outstanding report' given by me in two successive years. This raised the eyebrows of other members in the Committee. They asked our Director how only the persons working in the library of IAT were consecutively getting outstanding grades in their Annual Confidential Reports (ACR), which is now called 'Annual Performance Appraisal Report' (APAR), and thereby promotion, while other establishments were not. The Director convinced them by citing the procedure stipulated for writing the ACR. Under the set procedure, as Dean and Head of the Institute, he had to rely on the assessment given by the officer who initiated the report (IO) and the officer who reviewed (RO) it and graded it. Since the persons reported upon were directly working under the IO and the RO, they were the ones who had direct knowledge of their performance. The Dean had to go by their assessment, as he had no direct interaction with the persons reported upon to asses their performance. As Director, he had to satisfy himself that the grading was supported by facts and justification, and there was no apparent bias on the part of the IO and the RO towards the candidate reported upon. Since the outstanding grading report relating to IAT library candidates, which was before them recorded in detail the justification by testifying to the exemplary nature of performance by the candidates, he as Director was left with no choice but to concur with the grading given.

The criteria applied by me in grading a given work performance as 'outstanding' and the path to achieve it by the employee is explained here. The annual performance of an employee in the central government at that time was graded as poor, average, good, very good and outstanding, depending on the assessment of their work throughout that year. The problem arises in grading the assessment of performance as 'outstanding' and 'poor'. Since library and information activities constitute a service, applying physical or monetary criterion, such as relative efficiency and increase in output does not give a true picture of the contribution made by the employees as outstanding. An appropriate criterion to decide the outstanding nature of the performance of a candidate is to look for components such as innovation, addition to existing knowledge base, initiating new services or devices that make substantial impact on the users/ organization. These are the features that distinguish outstanding achievement from that of routine or ordinary performance. Any outstanding performance involves accepting challenges and making use of existing opportunities. Generally, it falls on the leader to pick the challenging task or a unique project that adds to the value of the library, and provide the opportunity to the individual worker to show his outstanding ability in achieving it. If it is a group venture, the outstanding contribution of an individual is to be decided by applying the criterion of how critical is the contribution of that particular member to the success of the project or the nature and amount of responsibility and creativity shouldered by the member. The following contributions give an idea of what was graded as 'outstanding' in my perception: Course on Information for Defence Scientists conducted by IC&L (see 8.2); setting of manpower standards for information centres and libraries (see 3.91), Computer application in IAT library (see 12.4 b); Mr. Desai and Mr. Raghuraman's exceptional skills in fulfilling users' expectations (see 7.2).

Managerial insight : Any performance to be graded as 'outstanding' has to be supported by proof. It must stand the scrutiny by knowledgeable persons in the field and the end users. The manager has an important role in creating opportunities to enable persons working under him to apply his or her knowledge, skill and ability to bring in excellence to the task/work which is unique and not routine in nature. Such contributions must result in great value addition or enormous savings to the organization through innovative means, thereby enhancing the quality and range of services provided by the library to the users. It is also a part of a manager's responsibility of taking care of the career prospects of such members working with him or her. It is the outstanding performances of co-workers that build up the reputation of the unit/organization, and adds to its brand value. In the process, the manager's reputation also gets enhanced.

(b) Assessment by Reverse Mode : Performance assessment of employees is an essential audit conducted in all organizations. The prime objective of performance audit is to judge whether the employee who is assessed is fit to continue in the job, if not what actions need to be taken, and to take care of employees' genuine career prospects in the organization. Whatever be the assessment mechanism put in place, the immediate higher line authority of the employee who is being assessed has an important say in the matter. As described above in the central government, in earlier years, the assessment process consisted of Annual *Confidential Report (ACR) Writing.* ACR for every employee was initiated by his or her immediate higher line authority called the Initiating Officer. The assessment report written by the Initiating Officer was reviewed by the next higher authority in the chain of command, called Reviewing Officer, and was finally completed by the Head of the establishment. The chain of command in the IAT library for ACR writing was made-up of the Director and Dean—Deputy Dean—Head, IC&L —- senior/ junior officers—non officers. Being the Head of IC&L, I was the reviewing officer for non officer cadre and initiating officer for the officer cadre working in the library. Thus, it was a 'from top to bottom' process. However, I was curious to get the reverse view, i.e. what the persons working with me thought about my performance as Head of Library.

To get the assessment from the bottom layer, I called a meeting of all members working with me in the rank of junior officers, assistants/junior librarians and below, and spelled out my desire. I requested them to be frank and forthright in expressing their assessment of my performance. I had also assured them that any negative assessment given by them would be taken by me in a sportive sprit, without getting biased against the person for his or her adverse assessment. I was disappointed at the response, as it appeared to me that barring one colleague (Mr. M.B. Patil), modesty prevented others to come out with their critical evaluation. Mr. Patil's assessment was that in situations involving a serious error, my dealing with the concerned persons tended to be intolerant and harsh that too exhibited in public. He was right, and I really appreciated his pointing out my fault.

Managerial insight : Everybody may commit mistakes, even serious ones, at one time or the other while in service. Pointing out the mistakes or shortcomings of subordinates, and suggesting remedial measures is different from display of rude behaviour, that too in public. The same could be done in private. No one has the right to humiliate his or her teammates, even when they are wrong.

(c) Probation Completion Review : The terms of service at the first entry point in a grade in the Government of India in most cases include the condition of successful completion of probationary period of one or two years. Based on the report of evaluation of one's performance during that period, he or she may be confirmed for continuing in the post, the service may be terminated, or the period of probation may be extended. The following is the account of completion of my probation period at IAT.

One day, the PA to the dean informed me that the Dean, wanted me to see him at ten o'clock in the morning next day. When I entered his chambers, I found that the Chairman, Library Committee- my immediate higher reporting authority was also present. The Dean, holding a file in his hand, remarked to me, "Do you know why I have called you? I am writing your probationary report". My response was a mere "Yes Sir". He then posed two questions to me, and wanted my explanation. The issues were related to: my not paying 'barrack damage'; and my not supporting promotion for Mr. Manikar (name changed) serving in the library. My responses to the two issues were:

Payment of Barrack Damage : Barrack damage is an amount imposed by the Military Engineering Service (MES)- the building and service maintenance agency, on the Institute for damages caused to the buildings and installations, for which no single individual can be held accountable. It cannot be paid from public funds. It is to be met by some other means. The Dean, probably after discussing with one or two senior civilian scientists, unilaterally decided to collect the amount from the officers of the establishment on a sharing basis. It came as a diktat. I was one of the very few officers who had refused to pay barrack damage as a matter of principle. The Dean asked me why I had not paid the barrack damage. I clarified that I had not paid it as it constituted penalizing me for the damages not caused by me or my colleagues in the library. He then, in a softened tone, explained that it was a cooperative means of solving the problem and would appreciate cooperation from all officers. Then, I said, in that case I had no objection in paying the amount, and I did pay immediately.

A Case of Undeserving promotion : The Dean asked me why I was against Mr. Manikar's (name changed) promotion. The background for this question was that Mr. Manikar was working as a library assistant in the library for many years. He never applied himself to work. Most of the time he used to be away from the library telling that his presence was required at the dean's office premises to look after garden related work.

This had gone on for many years. On my taking over the library, I was trying to put an end to his irresponsible behaviour.

I had also received an indirect hint that the Dean wanted him to be promoted to the next higher grade. In reply to his question I pointed out that Maniker's is a fit case for terminating his service and not that of giving a promotion. After I explained the facts relating to him, the meeting ended. My probationary report sailed through smoothly. Mr. Manikar left the organization thereafter. However, I could not make out what was the intention of the dean to link my probation report with the two issues.

Managerial insight : The exercise of authority alone does not solve all problems. The best way of solving certain types of problems, where the individual's cooperation is voluntary, is to take the affected parties into confidence, and try to make them understand that the designed remedy is in the larger good of the community. In the case of library assistant, the proverb "a stitch in time saves nine" aptly applies. If timely action was taken earlier to make him realize that indiscipline would not be tolerated, the situation would not have gone out of control. It is not in the interest of the organization that higher authorities create a situation, even indirectly, that encourages indiscipline.

7. A TOP CLASS ASSESSMENT MODEL

Of all the interviews in which I was either a candidate or a member of the Selection Board, one I faced at the Ahmedabad Textile Industries Research Association (ATIRA), Ahmedabad was unique. This interview took place in 1958. The post for which I had appeared as a candidate was that of Librarian, a fairly senior position in the organization. It was a four part selection process consisting of: a) written test, b) open discussion session, c) preliminary interview, and d) final interview in which only the Director and his deputy were present. The first three stages were common to all candidates. Only two candidates, including me, were called for the final interview. The selection of candidates for the final interview with the Director was made on the basis of overall performance of each candidate in the written test, discussion and preliminary interview. I also learnt that in the first three stages of the selection process the selection panel included a behavioural psychologist and a communication expert. I was selected for the post.

This interview was unique in other ways too. The interview

atmosphere was such that all the candidates appearing before the Selection Board were made to feel at home. The interview was conducted in the most professional way that one could think of. They had also arranged for tea before the preliminary interview, and lunch for those who were selected for the final interview. An interesting point was that all the candidates appearing for the interview were paid their to and fro railway fare, except me. It turned out that the candidate selected finally for the post, and issued with the appointment letter, was not entitled to reimbursement of travel fare, if the person declined the offer of appointment. I had declined their offer of appointment. This fact was indicated in their advertisement, which I had overlooked.

Managerial insight : Conducting an interview for the selection of candidates most suited for the organization is not an easy task. It calls for a professional approach. The process of selection described above looks near ideal. It is not easy to follow this model as it involves expenditure of large amount of time and resources, but ensures selection based on the assessment of the whole personality of a candidate, which is made up of his or her professional, psychological and managerial abilities to suit the requirements of the post.

REFERENCES

1. Srinivasan, Vidhya. Crack that job interview. The Hindu, Oct.6, 2014, p.15. (Educationplus).
2. Sharma, Ritwik. Avoiding referral programme landmines. Business Standard. 25 April 2016. P. 4
3. Zimmerman, Eilene. The groundwork for good references. *The Hindu*, May 8, 2013, p.7. (Original source: New York Times News Service).
4. Business Standard 10 July, 2013, p.9.(Technology). Sourcing talent by using online social professional network+ "background check of new hires".
5. Pradeesh Chandran. Out of favour, the Bell tolls no more! The Hindu, April 11, 2016, p.16.
6. Cappelli, Peter and Tavis, Anna. The Performane Management Revolution. Harvard Business Review. October 2016.

3

Projects, Operations And Accountability

Usually, when we talk of projects and programs our immediate thought goes to large-scale projects such as aerospace, irrigation and power, manufacturing, communication and roads, community development, educational development, health care system, public distribution of services and the like. This need not be so. In everyday organizational life we do undertake a number of small chores and tasks of limited scope, which also need thinking, planning, marshalling of resources, organizing, controlling and time scheduling.

Operations are taken to mean performance. Performance is how the personnel employed in an organization actually carry out the tasks or projects assigned to them. It is linked with the assigned position, or the job or the project. Operations have different aspects, such as production, controlling, testing and evaluation, financial, maintenance, marketing or delivery of service and others. There is a direct relationship between the position and the nature of operation; and between the position and the responsibilities to be discharged by the person holding the position. As operations in an organization are conducted by human beings, human weaknesses and strengths play a predominant part in managing operations and dealing with persons operating the system. Thus trust, use of tact, strategic thinking, ability to judge people and situations, acts of vindictiveness, pressure from unwarranted quarters, vested interests, and issues arising out of personality/ego clashes, differing perceptions about persons, policies and values are some of the features that crop up while managing operations and operational staff. Narrated here are experiences of the author relating to select projects/operations met with in managing two large libraries and information centres, the problems and obstacles faced and how they were overcome, as well as innovations and value addition steps taken to improve or extend the services.

1. PROJECTS AND PROGRAMS- PLANNING AND IMPLEMENTATION

A project is any undertaking, conducted to accomplish pre-set objectives within a set timeframe. A pilot project is a project undertaken to establish its feasibility and is experimental in nature. A program is a scheme, generally of limited duration, like arranging a conference, conducting a training activity and the like. The project on Digitalization of Information Resources of ADE Knowledge Centre is analyzed here. The other projects and programs that I dealt with, namely: a) Union Catalogue of Periodicals (INSDOC). In this, my role was limited to complete the ongoing project following the already set procedures. I had to leave the organization before its completion, after training my successor, b) Computerization of IAT library resources (see 12.4b, c) The Union List of Serials of DRDO libraries in the Bombay region (in digital form)- an extension of b), and d) Information Course for DRDO Scientists and Engineers (see 8.2) have already been described.

(a) Digitalization of ADE Knowledge Centre : How this project seized by the Computer Centre failed to fructify has been narrated in 3.5. Subsequently, the project was taken up by me as a challenge. The main hurdle in initiating the project came from none other than the Director of the Establishment. He was not willing to provide a computer to the KC. However, I succeeded in getting a computer allotted to KC only after a good deal of persuasion with Wg.Cdr. Bansal (name changed), the officer assigned with the task of distributing computers. Fortunately for me, I happened to know him well as we were contemporaries in IAT earlier. The most interesting point was that when we had advanced well in the project, the very Director who had refused to give a computer to KC brought a visiting VIP from the H.Q. to show the project under development. The VIP was impressed with the project and its progress. He was keen to know when the project would be completed. When I told him that it would take about 18 months, he wanted to know why it should take such a long time. I had to explain that the work was done by the existing staff of KC without any additional hands sanctioned to the project. Though library software packages were commercially available, it was developed by a creative software engineer working in Computer/Control Engineering division of the establishment, thus saving substantial amount of money and efforts. The project was successfully completed six months before the set target date.

Managerial insight : The above episode proves how valid is the proverb 'where there is a will there is a way.' A challenge often serves as a great motivator. In estimating the time required for completing a project one can set: a) an optimistic time frame, b) a pessimistic time frame, and c) the most likely time or realistic time frame. Often, one uses the optimistic time to impress the authorities to get the project sanctioned; pessimistic time as a cover to overcome criticism in case of any inordinate delay in completing the project; and the most likely time frame for self guidance. In the above instance I had given the pessimistic time as I was sure that the project would be completed within the most likely time. In giving the optimistic time there is a chance of coming under severe pressure from the higher authorities to still shorten the optimistic time to impractical levels, without providing required additional facilities/resources.

(b) Use of Barcode in Libraries : One of the items which impressed me when I visited America under the Fulbright program was the use of barcode system employed by American libraries for identifying publications. This brought accuracy in maintaining records, simplified issue and returns counter management, and saved time. I wanted to introduce this system in the Knowledge Centre of ADE. This remained an unfulfilled desire as I left the organization before completing my full tenure.

2. OPERATIONS

(a) 'Library shift' : The Institute of Armament Studies (IAS), renamed as the Institute of Armament Technology (IAT) in 1967, and now the Defence Institute of Armament Technology (a deemed university), started functioning in the premises of the College of Military Engineering (CME) at Dapodi, Poona in 1952. As the Institute grew, it needed its own campus. The new campus is located at Girinagar at a distance of about 25 km from Pune city. There is a story behind the selection of the new site. It is said that Air Vice-Marshal Mehra, the then Dean of IAS was searching for a suitable site for IAS.

Once, on a visit to the National Defence Academy at Khadakvasla, Poona, he was gazing over the surroundings. He was enchanted with the scenic beauty of the Khadakvasla lake facing the NDA and the placid surrounding area. There was sufficient open land on the opposite shore of the lake. Thus, it is said, he zeroed in on the place opposite NDA, on the other side of the lake, as the most suitable location for IAT. That is how the permanent campus for IAT was chosen. Shifting of an entire library from one location to another is not new. What is noteworthy here is that the operation of shifting was based on systematic planning following the principles of management—planning, organizing, staffing, leading and controlling. Shifting to the new site involved a distance of about 40 km from CME.

Planning and Organizing. The set objective was to shift the library to the new campus within 4 days and make the service available immediately thereafter. The plan consisted of preparing a blueprint of action, and the elements in the blueprint consisted of: survey of the new building and identifying the location of various sections and their internal arrangement; working out the resources required in terms of materials, manpower and transportation; chalking out detailed operational steps involved; selection of staff and allocation of tasks to each member; guiding the team to ensure that shifting and rearranging proceeded as envisaged; keeping ready an emergency plan in case of any breakdown; and keeping to the time schedule.

Execution : The mode of operation consisted of bundling books in each rack into lots of convenient size, numbering sequentially each bundle and the corresponding racks/shelves, so that while rearranging them in the new location, the existing order was replicated without confusion. At the new building the bundles were arranged according to their serial numbers and the books were re-shelved, thus retaining the original order The work was distributed and responsibility fixed by making each section head responsible for orderly transfer of his/her section and reassembling at the new premises. To ensure security, one person was detailed to accompany each truck/trip carrying the bundles. Only additional manpower sought was the help of a few labourers for tying the bundles, and for loading and unloading them from the trucks. The material requirement needed was stationery items and transportation service. Time schedule was worked out in advance for transportation and for rearrangement of the collection at the new location. The project was completed without any hitch, and the service restored as per planned time schedule.

Managerial insight : Translocating a library is nothing new. What is noteworthy here is that the entire operation was based on a blueprint prepared in advance following the basic principles of management, i.e., planning, organizing, staffing, leading and controlling.

(b) Extending Library Hours : The Bogey of Trade Union Opposition. Before my taking charge of ADE library, it used to remain closed to users during the morning and afternoon tea break period followed by the establishment. I felt that the library services should be accessible throughout the working hours of the establishment, and particularly during the three recess periods—breakfast, lunch and afternoon tea. The logic was that it is during these breaks that members are freer to visit the library and use it. When I discussed this issue with the Chairman, Library Committee and another member connected with the library, I was warned that earlier attempts to keep the library open during these breaks had failed due to strong opposition from the trade union of the establishment and also from library staff members. Hence, I should be prepared to face the consequences resulting from the decision to keep the service open during break periods.

There was no valid reason for the trade union to oppose

the move. On the part of the staff members there was the genuine reason of who was to manage the circulation counter during the break period. It was decided that it would be managed by rotation through mutual understanding. It was also made clear that there would be no written rotation schedule. The plan was put into operation from the very next day and it worked smoothly.

Managerial insight : Any plan of action based on pragmatic thinking that benefits the larger section of users will always be welcomed. There will be some genuine difficulties such as finding additional manpower, which can be sorted out, if the accrual of benefit outweighs the input cost. One must also take into account the general human psychology that any introduction of change is bound to cause some initial opposition to the change.

(c) Ad hoc Shifting of Library : The library building of IAT was designed with the proviso of two mezzanine floors to take care of future expansion. The need for extra floor space arose after fifteen years. It was decided to add on the mezzanine floors. Hence, it became necessary to vacate the two existing main floors so that the construction could be started. The problem for the library was where to accommodate the two sections without dislocating the services in a major way. Mr. Desai, my colleague, the three Section Heads and I, after carefully considering the available alternatives, came to the conclusion that the best possible way out was to accommodate the books, reports, and journals in the lobby of the library and its annex. Air Cdr. S. K. Nair, the then Director and Dean, instructed that we must hand over the two floors to the Military Engineering Service (MES) to begin their construction work. He suggested that he would allot two large halls in the main building to accommodate the two sections. I told him that we would manage within the existing premises, thus causing least discomfort to the readers. He left the decision to me telling "as head of library you know what is best." If we had moved the two sections to the main building, it would have resulted in managing two units differently located and far away from the main unit. This would have resulted in total dislocation of services due to many problems-administrative, as well as physical movement resulting from operating from two different locations.

After shifting the books, reports and journals as we had planned, the two floors were handed over to the MES. It took about nine months for the MES to construct the two mezzanine floors. All through that period the library functioned with least disturbance to the users of the library. The Dean was a regular user of the library even when it was functioning under ad hoc conditions, and hence could directly assess the functioning of the library. One day, after the library started functioning in the renovated building, I met the Dean as he was coming to the library. The first thing he did was to congratulate me for managing the library so well with minimal dislocation of services. It was a happy moment for all of us working in the library.

Managerial insight : A genuine appreciation of the task well accomplished serves as an invaluable incentive. It creates a sense of responsibility in the recipient worker to strive continuously to retain that trust. Not many leaders are bestowed with that quality of mind.

3. QUALITY Vs. COST

Additional space in the form of two mezzanine floors added to the library building needed additional racks with book shelves. The MES, which was to arrange for the racks, asked us to accept the racks manufactured by local manufactures as their prices were comparatively low, rather than go by standard manufacturers like Godrej & Boyce who specialized in manufacturing library racks. The existing racks were of Godrej make. We had serious doubts about the quality of the steel racks of other makes, which was confirmed by the bad experience of libraries that had gone in for racks other than Godrej make. Hence, I insisted on Godrej shelving. The Library Committee strongly supported our stand. The issue was referred to the MES. A meeting was called by Air Cdr Nair, the Dean, to sort out the issue, which was attended by the Engineer-in-chief (CE), MES (who had arrived from Delhi), and myself.

In the meeting, I insisted on Godrej furniture because of its quality, and the risk involved in going in for untested manufacturers, just because the latter had quoted lower prices. The Chief Engineer made the point that when the country was producing sophisticated items required by the defence department, how could one say that other manufacturers would not be able to produce a simple item like library racks. I countered, asking why most people preferred to buy a Godrej refrigerator, when other brands with same capacity and features were available in the market with a lower price-tag. The Director concluded that since the librarian, who was responsible for managing the library, insisted on standard quality, it was better to go in for Godrej make. The CE pointed out that the library would have to wait for a year or two to get the Godrej stacks as they had to get a special sanction. When the Director asked me whether we could wait for two years, I said that we would. The meeting ended requesting the CE to get the necessary sanction. The library got the Godrej shelves in about eight months, under one-time exception made by the H.Q.

Managerial insight : Only a leader of high caliber can appreciate a just stand taken by his or her subordinates, and support that stand. It is better to go in for standard items rather than untested ones, just because they are cheaper. The opposite party can be convinced if our reasoning is sound, based on facts, and if we have no vested interests. In the long run quality works out more economical. Here, the pertinent question to be asked is whether the intended trade off between the cost and the quality is justified in the long run?"

4. A LIGHT BRUSH WITH THE TRADE UNION

My first experience with a trade union sponsored strike came when I was in Jamshedpur working in the Tata Iron and Steel Co. The call for the strike was given by the recognized trade union of the industrial establishment. It was quite an experience seeing the psychology of workers and the attitude of the management. The good thing was that there was no violence but only slogan shouting at the gates. The strike was a success as far as the workers' participation was concerned. The technical and managerial staff did not participate. I attended the library in spite of threats, which were not serious in nature. I did receive a commendation letter for loyalty from the top management for attending work on the day of the strike.

My real brush with the local worker's union came when I was in ADE. One morning, two large size posters were pasted at the entrance to the library, which read "Down with..... and his autocratic behaviour towards union members." I did not bother about it. I had no idea why the Union had taken such a stand against me. On the next day or so a union representative came to me accompanied by another member- a user of the library and demanded to know why the library was collecting late fee on books not returned within the due date only from the workers. I explained that the rule of late fee imposition was framed to ensure that every user of the library got an equal opportunity to borrow every book in the library; and it was enforced uniformly without exception. I also showed him the copy of the receipt of late fee collected from a senior officer to prove that the rule was applied equally to all. I also told them that if they were still not convinced with my explanation they must give in writing their complaint so that the issue could be discussed by the Library Committee for review. The issue stopped at that.

The All India Central Government Employees' Strike: Another experience with the trade union sponsored strike also happened while I was in ADE. The Federation of Central Government Employees' trade unions had given a call for an all India strike. The strike was almost total. The local union representatives had effectively blocked the entry to the establishment. Tension was all around. The situation was such that anytime violence could erupt. Since it was an all India strike, I had anticipated trouble in reaching office on the day of strike by taking the usual route of journey. Hence I had moved to a lodge near the establishment so that I could reach the gate well in advance. But it was not to be, as workers had completely blocked the entry at the gates. In the hope that I would get the necessary protection to enter, I telephoned the establishment's security authorities. They washed off their hands. If officers are not given protection, are they to risk their lives? The officers attendance was the lowest in ADE compared to other DRDO establishments in Bangalore and elsewhere. This reflected badly on the management of the establishment, which it seems, was conveyed to the top management.

Managerial insight : There is a general perception that all trade union activities are anti-establishment and anti-executive. This is not always true unless the issues are related to workers' economic interests or meting out unwarranted harsh treatment to workers. Many times explaining the situation truthfully will solve the problems pertaining to individual units or specific individuals, provided there is no cause for doubting the integrity and honesty of the concerned head of the unit in the mind of the other party. When political parties take control of workers' union, conflict resolution gets vitiated and becomes difficult to resolve at the personal/local level.

5. THE DIGITALIZATION PLAN THAT FAILED TO TAKE OFF

One morning there was a call from the Director's Office intimating me that there was a meeting at the Director's office and I should be present. I couldn't make out why the meeting was called. When I went to the meeting there was the Director, and the Head of Computer Centre (HCC) - an independent unit housed within ADE campus, accompanied by his Senior Scientific Assistant. The Senior Assistant had worked with me earlier in IAT, Poona. The Director told me that HCC was entrusted with the task of computerizing the library functions of ADE, and I must spare the services of a senior assistant exclusively to help them. He also instructed that I must submit a weekly report on the progress made. I was aghast at this development. I felt that courtesy demanded that I was at least taken into confidence before imposing the decision, since the responsibility of managing the IC&L rested with me. I expected that at least now the HCC would discuss with me to ascertain the needs of the library that are to be met while designing the software. No such discussion took place. On my part, I spared the services of a library staff member to work with them. For a week or so the Senior Assistant used to spend some time in the library talking to junior staff members about computerization of the catalogue function. Once or twice he met me briefly, which was more of a courtesy call rather than work related. Since the work had not even started, my first weekly report to the Director was that of nil progress. The report also highlighted the need for ensuring compatibility of the software they were to develop with other systems in operation in DRDO, and also to keep in mind the existing standards on the subject, as the HCC did not seem to be aware of it. Subsequent weekly reports also reflected nil progress as there was hardly any progress. This went on for eight weeks or so, by which time I left for USA for six months under the Fulbright Fellowship. When I returned, I saw the whole exercise had ended abruptly as it had begun. I was also told that HCC did not get the required cooperation from the library because of their overbearing attitude towards the Chairman, Library Committee, who was in overall charge of the library in my absence. An interesting part of this episode is that the HCC was one of the early people to congratulate me on my receiving the *Scientist of the Year Award – 1983*, in recognition of my work on computer application for the first time in IAT library and DRDO.

Managerial insight : Technology expertise and the requirements of the unit or discipline where it is to be applied constitute two distinct parts of any technology application plan. Unless the technology specialist understands the requirements of the user and the purpose to be served in all its detail, dovetailing technology becomes difficult. It is incumbent on the operational manager to clearly explain his requirements and the relevant intricacies of the field of operation to the technology provider. Unless these two conditions are met, technology implementation is unlikely to become a full success. Ultimately, it is the operational manager who is to deliver the service. Hence, it is imperative on the part of the decision-making authorities on technology application to take into confidence the operational manager from the initial stage itself, which was missing in this case.

6. INNOVATION AND PROBLEM SOLVING

When we think of innovation and problem solving in an organizational context, invariably what comes to mind is creating new products or adding value to existing gadgets and services often with fancy names, or increasing productivity in the organization. This need not be so. In everyday functioning we face problems- big and small, and difficult situations which can be overcome by applying creative thinking or adapting solutions that already exist but about which we are not aware, or by simple experiments. Two such cases are stated here.

(a) Fungal Attack on Books : For the first time, in the monsoon season of 1975, IAT library located on one side of the Khadakvasla Lake was faced with the serious problem of wide-spread fungus attack on books and bound journals, particularly affecting the spine. An interesting point was that the fungus problem was not faced by the library of the Central Water and Power Research Station (CWPRS) located about 2 km away from IAT. The two institutions shared the same environment in terms of geographic and meteorological features, such as altitude, landscape, vegetation, rainfall, temperature, and humidity. Search in the literature to know the cause was not of much help. Hence, we had to find a solution to the problem ourselves. It was taken up as a scientific research problem by the library, conducted in a laboratory environment. Of course, it required application of rigorous scientific method, perseverance and interaction with the India Meteorological Department, CWPRS, and the Hindustan Antibiotics Ltd.—all located in Pune. It was established that sterilization of the stack rooms with four to five sprays of 10% solution of thymol (para-di-chloro benzene) in methyl alcohol at an interval of 20 days during monsoon season eradicated the fungal menace. The fungus was found to belong to the genus *aspergillus*. The findings of the research work were later published[1].

(b) Improving Upon Stock Verification Process : Conducting annual verification of stock is a compulsory requirement in all government libraries. The task is tedious, time consuming, and necessitates closing of the library for users during stock taking period. However, it provides an opportunity to attend to house-keeping operations, such as weeding out dead stock, rectification of shelf arrangement, indication of missing books and updating of loan records. The verification work is conducted by a team made up of members drawn from departments outside the library. The library of IAT used to be closed for 10 to 15 days during stock-taking, which was unacceptable. Hence, there was a need for studying the process in depth and evolve an efficient procedure particularly keeping in mind the need to reduce the closure of the library to 3 to 4 days. The study consisted of analyzing the methods followed in eight yearly stock-takings and improving each method by introducing changes for subsequent stock-taking. The method finally arrived at resulted in optimum benefits, and they were:

1. Stock-taking of the library consisting of about 40000 items could be completed in 3 to 4 days;
2. The initial list of unaccounted books got reduced from 300 to 50 items depending on the care exercised during operation;
3. Reduction in errors caused due to human fatigue;
4. Proper record keeping of operation and accountability; and
5. Orderly conduct of stock-taking.

The study described here, and later published in a journal, is entirely based on manual processes[2]. Tallying (and even sensing the label writing) part of the work can now be entrusted to computer; and thereby save enormous time, human labour, reduce errors and possibly avoid closure of library for stock verification.

Managerial insight : In all activities/functions in an organization one faces some problems at one time or another. There is always scope for economizing of efforts and improving upon the existing mode of operation. Creative thinking helps in finding solutions to problems. Application of innovative ideas enriches an organization. A beneficial application of innovation in an organization has to be centered on solving the problem on hand and enrich its worth. The positive impact of innovations/ research may take the form of immediate or long range benefit. There is a gulf between arriving at innovative ideas and their successful application in live situations. Most successful applications of innovative ideas involve an element of risk. A successful manager encourages innovation and is not afraid of taking risks, within limits, in adopting the innovation. The adoption of an innovative idea in a group task calls for proper briefing of all participants in the project on the steps involved in applying the new idea/method, their importance, and the role of each member of the group. It is a responsibility of a good manager to identify talent and make use of that talent to the benefit of the organization.

(c) Substitution of Book Labels : Call number writing on the spine of books is mostly done by pasting labels and writing call numbers on it. This two stage process of pasting and writing is tedious and consumes more time. With passage of time and use, the writing gets smudged and reading letters becomes difficult. How to overcome this problem called for some new thinking. As a consequence, it was decided to try writing directly on the spine of a book eliminating the use of label. Replacing ink by suitable white paint seemed to work well. One problem in using paint was its permanency. Sometimes it becomes necessary to change the call number of a book when it needs to be reclassified. In such instances permanency of paint becomes a hindrance. This problem is overcome by rubbing the written surface with the help of a soft tissue dipped in turpentine/petrol which dissolves the paint and makes the spine surface ready for rewriting. The new method was introduced to solve the label problem.

Managerial insight : In general, it can be said that there is always a better way of doing a thing. The problem with some of us is that we do not think. It also requires a mind that observes and questions. If we think deeply and creatively a solution to a problem always appears. Innovations need not always be centered round the theme of enhancing profit or beating competitiveness. Anything that reduces drudgery, adds value or enhances aesthetics to a prevailing process or product or service constitutes a welcome innovation. Many of the innovative ideas are simple. It looks simple only after the idea is properly implemented and proves a success.

7. ROB PETER TO PAY PAUL ? THE QUESTION OF ETHICS

The financial year end was nearly two months away. It was the time to take stock of the book fund expenditure at the ADE Knowledge Centre. A few invoices amounting to a large total received from another local book supplier were the only pending major bills on hand. These bills pertained to books supplied on "approval" basis. However, books costing nearly the same amount ordered with M/s Samarth Subscription Agency, Pune (SSA) were expected to materialize in 4 to 6 weeks. These books were specifically ordered and the firm had to import them directly from abroad, which meant additional efforts and expenses to the firm. Other than SSA none of the other firms were willing to entertain orders for supply of books which needed importing by them. Given this background, the library was morally bound to give precedence in payment to the SSA over the other firm. Otherwise, SSA had to wait until May next year. The other firm was told to wait until April/May of next year. The other firm brought pressure through the Chairman, Library Committee to pass its bills immediately. When the matter was raised in the Library Committee by the Chairman, I stood my ground. It was also pointed out that passing of bills is an executive function over which the Library Committee has no jurisdiction. I thought that was the end of the matter. But the Secretary of the Committee sent me the minutes of the meeting for my signature, which recommended immediate passing of the bills submitted by the other firm, in spite of my disagreement. After recording my note of dissent on the file, I put up the case to the Scientist-G, my immediate higher executive authority before it reached the Director, the final authority.

The Scientist- G returned the minutes to the Chairman, Library Committee asking for clarification in view of my note of dissent. The file came back to me with the explanation given by the Chairman. The explanation was that the firm M/s SSA would not be able to supply the books before the date set by the Finance Section for passing bills, and hence the amount would lapse, unless we passed the pending bills in hand. I had accounted for such an eventuality and the means of overcoming it. I sent back the file explaining that the matter was discussed in advance with the Finance officer, and he had committed to pass the bill as a special case even if it was submitted after the due date. Scientist-G concurred with my stand. The ordered books arrived in time and the question of making it a special case did not arise. The other firm had to wait till the next financial year.

Managerial insight : When there is vested interest or ego problem, rational or wise thinking will be the first casualty. Even in management one has to give due consideration to uphold the ethical values, wherever they may be involved. Overriding ethical values may bring in short term gains, but adversely affect the organization's long term interests. Decisions based on personal interests as against organizational interests are bound to adversely affect the service and harm the brand name/ reputation of the organization/unit, in this case the ADE Knowledge Centre. Usurpation of executive power vested in the library manager by an advisory body like the Library Committee is detrimental to the proper functioning of library and information services, which is not in the interest of the organization.

8. TACKLING IGNORANCE AT THE TOP

It was my early days at IAT. One day the Dean of the Institute came to the library on an inspection visit. After the inspection he made the observation that by making the books stand vertically on the shelves, they get physically weakened and get damaged. He asked me to get the shelving mode changed, by repositioning the books so that each book rests horizontally on its spine. I was aghast at the order, but kept mum. Common sense told that by making a book stand horizontally along its spine, identifying it becomes impossible as the title/ author of the book and it's '*Call number*' label pasted on the spine will not be visible. As the incident took place in the first few days of my joining the Institute, I felt it was better not to contradict him at the first encounter. I was also sure that he would realize soon the impracticality of his suggestion, and would not press for its execution. That was exactly what happened. When he came on his second visit to the library after a month or so he never raked up the issue again. That was the end of it. It may be of interest to know that in military service, it is said that generally, a higher officer does not like to hear a 'NO' from the subordinates at the first instance. It is fine to say the same 'NO' subsequently.

Managerial insight : Occasionally one may be faced with situations where one's superior authority, out of ignorance, may come up with instructions that are unworkable or even insensible. In handling such situations having some patience and employing a little diplomacy on the part of the manager will make him or her see through as the other person would have realized his or her mistake by then.

9. THE BLAME GAME

One day, the library received a note from the General Staff Officer (GSO of IAT) wanting to know what action had been taken to procure the textbook mentioned in the enclosed Minutes of the recent Academic Council Meeting. The context in which the textbook entered the picture was that the Academic Council was discussing the poor performance of students in a particular subject. Prof. Probit Sen (name changed), the Head of the concerned Faculty attributed the reason for poor performance of students in the concerned subject to the non-procurement of the stated textbook by the library. It was a clear case of the Faculty trying to cover up its lapse by putting the blame on the library.

The fact was that the Faculty had put the indent on the library to procure a large number of copies (about 50 in number) of the text book only recently. The library was not informed of the urgency of procurement. The titled publication being a high cost specialized scientific work with limited demand, the distributors/book shops in India holding the publication in their ready stock was a remote possibility. It was to be specifically imported from USA which normally took 6 to 8 weeks. The library had placed the order immediately on receipt of the demand. The copies were expected to arrive in about 3 weeks. These facts were communicated to the GSO. A copy of this communication was also sent to the Chairman of the Academic Council, and to the Head of the concerned Faculty. The library on its part asked the supplier to procure the copies expeditiously.

Managerial insight : Making others scapegoats for one's failures does not always pay. But then, by adopting this unethical strategy sometimes people try to get out of a hot situation, particularly when the other party is not there to defend itself or expose the falsehood. One day or the other the facts come out. A good leader accepts his or her lapses rather than pass on the blame to others. It is a part of managerial ethics, and a factor in creating trust and respect.

9.1. People Living in Glass Houses Shouldn't throw Stones at Others

Framing Manpower Norms for Libraries. One of the issues that came up for discussion at the Meeting of Heads of DRDO Libraries and Technical Information Centres (TIC) held in Delhi in 1980 was the need for framing manpower norms for DRDO libraries. The staff norms for libraries available at that time were the ones formulated by Dr. S.R. Ranganathan, the University Grants Commission (UGC) and the Documentation Research and Training Centre (DRTC), Bangalore. The new developments in the field and the changed pattern of information services called for a fresh look at the manpower standards for libraries and information centres. The task of framing the norms was assigned to a Committee headed by a senior DESIDOC member. Since DESIDOC had not made any progress the work was entrusted in 1981 to L&IC of IAT. Following a novel concept of a *standard library unit*, manpower norms for libraries were evolved taking into account the current and changing needs. The draft of the norms was sent to all the DRDO libraries requesting them to try out the formulae at their units and send their feedback. Most of the libraries sent their comments, except DESIDOC.

DESIDOC being the largest documentation centre covering all the functions expected of a central unit, their feedback was essential to finalize the standard. Even after reminders there was no response from them. Just about a month before the next conference was due, where the issue of staff norms would come up for discussion, the Director, DESIDOC wrote a semiofficial letter to the Director, IAT complaining that IAT had not come out with the standards. The Director forwarded that letter to me for replying. A detailed letter was prepared stating the fact that it was DESIDOC's failure to respond to our communication even after reminders that had held up finalization of the manpower norms; and also stating the fact that IAT volunteered to take up the task after the central body was unable to handle the work. After receiving their feedback, we were able to finalize and submit the norms for discussion at the next conference. The new standard was pragmatic and received the general approval of the participants. The same was later published in a journal.[3]

Managerial insight : Dissonance between desire, ability and commitment stands in the way of accomplishing a project or task in time. Before putting the blame on others for one's failure, it is necessary on the part of the blaming party to make a self introspection and accept responsibility. This would save later embarrassment.

REFERENCES

1. Narayana, G.J., Desai, H.G. and Joseph, L. (Mrs.). Fungal attack on books: A report. *Annals of Library Science and Documentation* 25 (1-4): 106-09, Mar.-Dec.1978.
2. Raghuraman, R.N., Meera G. Joshi and Narayana, G.J. Stock verification in the absence of shelf list. *Annals of Library Science and Documentation* 22(1):25-29, 1975.
3. Narayana, G.J., Desai, H.G. and Meera Joshi. Personnel standards for R&D libraries and information centres. *Library Science* 24(4):185-195, 1987.

4

Authority and Its Exercise

Authority is the power vested in a position and exercised by the person holding that position in discharging the assigned responsibilities. Success or failure of an organization or its constituent units/subunits depends to a large extent on how the mangers/leaders exercise the authority vested in them and discharge their duties and responsibilities. The responsibility lies in setting proper goals and realizing them. Improper exercise of authority is often traced to ignorance, immaturity, lack of ethics, selfishness, ego problems on the part of the persons holding the positions, and vague organization structure. Authority and accountability go together. Without making persons/executives holding authority accountable for their actions leads to chaos in the organization or passing the buck. Ensuring accountability injects the sense of responsibility in the minds of persons entrusted with the tasks/authority. Proper exercise of authority and insisting on accountability for the consequences of such an exercise are inherent features of effective management practice.

When a functionary holding authority entrusts his power and functions wholly or partly to some other functionary either for a short time or for a long period of time is called delegation of power. Such delegations could be the result of well thought out actions or dictated by exigencies. Ability to delegate authority in an effective manner is also an important component of good leadership. Not all managers have the right aptitude to delegate authority to their subordinate functionaries/ teammates. Often, one sees two tendencies in delegating power- managers who are excessively desirous of delegating authority and those who are loath to delegate. While the former leads to shirking of one's responsibility, as well as thrusting of additional work/ responsibility on other functionaries: and the latter results in trust deficit in the organization's culture and under utilization of employee talent. Striking a balance between the two extremes is the hallmark of an effective leader.

While non-exercise of one's authority where and when required is a failure of discharging one's duty, misuse use of one's authority constitutes a serious blemish. The former restricts employee development and leadership growth, the latter results in distrust and frustration among employees in the organization. Narrated here are a few instances of misuse of authority and their consequences.

1. MISUSE OF AUTHORITY: PURCHASE OF IRRELEVANT PUBLICATIONS

A note sent by the Dean asked the library to purchase a particular multi-volume title on Indian history. It was a high priced title costing a large amount even at that time i.e.1969/70. It was apparent, at the outset itself, that spending such a huge sum of money on the item, whose relevance to the Institute was doubtful, was not justified. After ascertaining the contents of the volumes, it was clear to me that the decision to purchase them was not justified as they had no relevance to either teaching or research activities of IAT. The note was returned to Dean stating that the volumes could not be purchased. The reaction of the Dean was clearly authoritative, antagonistic and vindictive in nature. The next day I was going out of the library, when I saw the Dean accompanied by his *stick orderly* (the military practice of a soldier holding an open sword leading the dignitary) coming to the Library, I returned to my Office. He entered my room, rage showing all over his face, and questioned me as to who I was to challenge his order to purchase the volumes. Here, the principle of delegation of authority came in handy to me. My reply was simple and straight. "Sir, it is the Standing Orders of the Institute (a written document codifying the rules and practices to be followed by the Institute). As per the Standing Orders the librarian is the exclusive authority, who has to certify to the Control of Defence Accounts (CDA), the pay master, that only those publications essential for the proper functioning of the Institute have been bought. Without that certificate the CDA will not pass the bill. It is clear from the titles and the contents of each volume that they fall outside the teaching and research activities of the Institute. Hence, I can not certify that the volumes are essential for the proper functioning of the Institute. I am answerable to the CDA and the government that public funds are utilized properly." He insisted on my obeying his order to purchase the volumes. In that case, I persisted, that he must send in writing the justification for the purchase of the volumes and its academic relevance to the Institute. Bitten by pride and self-interest he sent me in writing the justification by making out a case that the books deal with the topic of military strategy and tactics which is taught in some of the Courses. I was left with no option but to procure the volumes. The interesting part is that it turned out that his kin who was then studying for MA in history needed those books, rather than the courses. The only user who borrowed those volumes was the Dean. This episode did not end here. Its adverse repercussions on me are narrated in Sections .4 and .5 below.

Managerial insight : Conflicts arise in situations where there is dissonance between professional integrity of the librarian and lack of personal integrity on the part of the higher authorities involved in the situation. I had the satisfaction that I fulfilled my duty without compromising my professional integrity, irrespective of its consequences to me personally.

2. PURCHASE OF RELEVANT PUBLICATION: A CONTRASTING EPISODE

Directly in contrast to the above episode is the one experienced by me in a later year. Then the concerned authority was the late Air. Cdr. S. K. Nair (AVSM), the Dean. One day he walked into the library in search of a particular book on management. He did not find the book in the stacks and wanted to know whether the book was in the library. The library had not purchased that book. The title in question was a standard book on management, and a costly one, which the library ought to have had in its collection on Management. When I told him that we didn't have the title in our stock, and we would purchase the book, he categorically said that the library should not purchase the book. He made it clear that he would buy the book as it was needed for his daughter's use. The library did purchase a copy, but he never borrowed it.

Managerial insight : True leaders lead by example, and will never compromise with organizational interests and personal integrity.

3. PURCHASE OF PATENTS: LACK OF OVERALL JUDGMENT

A note from the Head of the Engineering Section of ADE asked the Knowledge Centre (KC) to subscribe to the Engineering series of the patents issued by an American patent publishing body. The annual subscription for the series amounted to about Rs. 50000, a huge amount at that time. The question was whether the subscription would yield justifiable value for money invested. A careful and unbiased evaluation of the demand showed that the number of patents of relevance to the R&D activities of the establishment out of the hundreds of patents covered by the annual subscription seemed to be about a dozen or so. It was clear that there was no valid justification for spending such a huge amount. Saying "No" was tricky, as the Section Head who had recommended the purchase was an influential person. The easier way out for me was to put the subscription proposal to the Library Committee or put up the file to the Scientist-G, to whom I was reporting, for his decision. The former option seemed to be a futile exercise, as the tendency is not to take a strong stand against an influential person; and the latter option would have resulted in compromising with the authority and abdicating responsibility vested in me as Head of Knowledge Centre. Putting up the requisition note to the Scientist-G also had the possible risk of his toeing the line of the indenter, even if he was convinced about the rightness of not subscribing to the title. Hence, I sent back the requisition stating that there was no justification for subscribing, and also indicating the reasons for not subscribing. At the same time it was made clear that the KC would procure specific patents that the Section needed. As far as KC was concerned, that was the end. However, I came to know later, that the Head of Section raised the issue informally with the Scientist-G, who stood by my stand.

Managerial insight : It is a case of professional integrity and discharging his duty on the part of the librarian. Asking for subscribing to the whole set of patents without a full evaluation shows lack of proper judgment in assessing the value return on money invested. Decision-making in such situations is often a test case for the librarian's professional integrity.

4. TRANSFER OF SSA: AN ACT OF VINDICTIVENESS

A direct result of my refusal to purchase the multi-volume book on Indian History narrated in Section 1 was the abrupt transfer of Mr. Patil, a Senior Scientific Assistant (SSA) working in the library to a Faculty dealing with a highly technological subject. The absurdity of the transfer was that Mr. Patil neither had qualified in the technological subject nor had any experience in that field. He was recruited specifically to work in the library, had qualified in Library Science, and all his professional experience was in the field of library and information science. He had not asked for a transfer. His transfer to the technology faculty, without providing a replacement to the library, was a sheer act of vendetta. It was unimaginable that before issuing the transfer order, the highest executive authority of the Institute did not bother to think (or did think but got blinded by emotion) what an employee having no knowledge of electronics would do in the Electronics Faculty. Since a cool evaluation of the situation showed me that the authorities would realize the folly of the transfer and act wisely sooner than later, I did not rake up the issue. However, it took nearly a month for the Dean to realize the absurdity of the transfer, and to post Mr. Patil back to the library as suddenly as he was transferred earlier.

Managerial insight : Any managerial decision taken out of sheer vindictiveness and without taking into account the decision's adverse impact on all stakeholders is sure to make the manager cut a sorry figure. Display of such an attitude is bound to demoralize the Head of the affected unit and the staff members working with him/her.

5. TRANSFER OF SERIALS PROCUREMENT FROM LIBRARY TO STORES SECTION

Procurement and processing of periodicals is an important function of libraries. Management of serials is a specialized function and librarians are trained in that. What happens if it is treated as any other store item, and the work is entrusted to Stores Manger? Why such a decision?

The library of IAT was functioning smoothly for years on. One day the library received an order from the Senior Administrative Officer (SAO) stating that as per the instructions of the Dean the function of ordering and receipt of journals and other serials was transferred to Stores Department. I could not make out the reason for such a sudden decision. The main reason behind this decision seemed to be my not cooperating with the Dean in procuring the multivolume title on Indian history (see 1 above).

I knew that shifting serials procurement to Stores section would result in chaos, raise accountability problems, duplication of efforts; and ultimately lead to disruption of service to the users of the library. The Stores Officer expressed to me that he had no role in the transfer decision, and he was only obeying the order; but it was known that he was in the Dean's confidential circle. Trying to convince the Senior Administrative Officer on the irrationality of the order and its negative consequences on the smooth functioning of the library had no desired impact. Since it was an administrative issue between the Dean and me, I felt that there was no point in taking the issue to the Library Committee. Following this conclusion, the relevant records pertaining to periodicals management were transferred to the Stores section. The newly arriving journal issues delivered to the library were sent to the Stores section for processing. Due to lack of knowledge and experience of handling serials, the Stores Department could not manage. The issues of periodicals began to pile up in the Stores. At the library end readers began to complain about the non-access to latest issues of journals. Very soon the Stores people realized that managing periodicals is not as simple as ordering a stores item. Within a week the order was rescinded.

Managerial insight : When changing an established procedure or the authority currently managing a task, the manager has to carefully weigh the pros and cons of introducing the desired change. The deciding authority has to ask first why the change is needed. Any change decision is to be based on rationality and pragmatism, and not on personal whims and hearsay. Instituting any change must result in improvement or value addition. A fundamental rule of good management is that before deciding a change, the decision-making authority has to take into confidence the persons/departments that will be affected by the intended change to avoid facing unpleasantness or humiliation later. In the present case this basic principle was given a go by.

6. ON A FAULT-FINDING MISSION

One day Dr.Vibuthi (name changed), the Director of ADE at that time came to the library and sent for me. He was in the books section. When I met him, he showed me a place of wrongly shelved book and asked me was it the way to maintain shelf arrangement. I replied that in an open access library occasionally such misplacements do take place and the staff is constantly at work to rectify such mistakes. Then he raised the topic of wrong classification of books. I was surprised at this. I asked him what he meant, to which he quoted the instance of wrong classification of books on 'fire *control system*' (see 9.3). I couldn't know how he came to know of this. I accepted that it was a mistake. I also explained that there were a few more books that were wrongly classified, and action was under way to rectify those mistakes. Instead of leaving the issue at that, he started not only leveling some vague charges against me, but started questioning my professional ability to manage and my integrity. I could then make out that he had come to the library with the sole intention of finding fault with me. What hurt me most was his questioning my professional integrity and managerial ability. The fact was that the book on fire control and a few other books wrongly classified were purchased and technically processed many years ago when the library was under Dr.Vibuthi's direct charge, during his earlier tenure in the establishment as head of a department. I forcefully brought out this fact to him with proof and told him, that if any one was to be held responsible for the wrong classification of those books then it would be him. Several readers who were in the library were staring at us. At once, he realized his weak position and left the premises directing me to see him immediately in his office.

I went to his office and waited for some ten minutes. There was no call from him. When I approached his Personal Assistant, he told me that I should wait for some more time. After asking the PA to telephone to me when the Director was free to see me, I returned to my office. An hour later I got the call and faced the Director in his office. He tried to corner me by asking why I was refusing short leave to some of the workers in the Reprographic Unit, which was under my control. I had not imagined that he would raise this topic, that too unexpectedly. I could not comprehend immediately the motive behind the question. Granting of short leave was not a right of the worker, but left to the discretion of the Section Head. My reply was that I had never refused short leave to any person in the unit when the request was genuine. It looked funny to me to hear him say that Dr.Mayur (name changed), the Deputy Director had brought to his notice my refusal to grant short leave. The shocking part of it was that Dr.Mayur had left the establishment some 18 months earlier, which meant that even if the charge was true, the Director was raking up the issue nearly one and a half years after the incident. Then we were engaged in a challenge of eye stare. I do not remember now, after a lapse of so many years, who blinked first. He also accused me of being proud. Probably, his vanity could not relish my uprightness and blemish-less career.

One of the outcomes of this encounter with the Director was his taking revenge on me. This came in the form of permanent cancellation of my membership in the Standing Committee on selection of officers for library and information positions in the DRDO establishments. It became evident from the communication I received from the H.Q. that their earlier letter requesting me to be present at the Selection Committee meeting, which was to take place a week later, stood cancelled. These aberrations and malfeasant acts of authorities in power do occur in the lives of organizations and individuals, and one has to put up with them. I have the satisfaction that in spite of a few aberrations like this I could contribute to the development of the library and raise its level to that of a Knowledge Centre, build a good team, and leave a good legacy.

Managerial insight : Vindictiveness coupled with arrogance of power and petty mindedness is the worst enemy of an administrator, not to speak of a leader. No amount of Public Relations efforts can cover up this deficiency. When such persons occupy the topmost executive post of an organization, the organization's interest will become the first casualty. It is the duty of a good manager to motivate persons working with him or her to perform in a manner that leads to excellent achievements *which makes them feel proud.*

7. A FAILED ATTEMPT TO USURP MANAGEMENT CONTROL OVER LIBRARY

How a power seeking officer unsuccessfully tried to grab control over the library is narrated here. The place was IAT, Pune and the parties were Cdr. Gomthi (name changed) from Navy, the Head of a Faculty, who had newly joined the Institute on the retirement of its earlier Head and me, the Head of Library and Information Centre. The narration presents the facts of the encounter that took place over the telephone but not necessarily the exact words used.

The telephone on my table rings, and I pick up the telephone.

"Hello! Is it the Chief librarian speaking?

Yes. I am the Chief librarian.

I am Cdr. Gomthi, Chairman, Faculty of... speaking.

Yes. Please tell me. What can I do for you?

Please come over to my office, I have some thing to discuss with you on library matters.

Sorry! I am busy with work. You are welcome to come over to the library.

The telephone is cut off at the other end, but rings again after ten minutes.

Hello, I am Cdr. Gomthi speaking again.

Yes! Please tell me?

(In a raised tone) How can you refuse to come to my office when I want to discuss some important matters pertaining to library? You know library comes under my administrative control. (It took me a couple of seconds to grasp the significance of his last sentence implying that he was my boss.)

Sorry. I am busy with some important work. I can not come. You are welcome to come over to library to discuss the issue. As far as your control over library is concerned, there is no such order issued. If and when it comes in the *Daily orders* of the Institute, let me see.

Please hear me. There is no need for it to come in the *Daily orders*. You know the library was under Dr..., my predecessor. I am now heading that Faculty, and hence the library also comes under my charge.

Sorry! Being Head of the Faculty of..., does not imply ipso facto transfer of control over library to you. Dr....exercised control over library not by virtue of his being the Head of the Faculty, but by being the Deputy Dean, the senior most among the Heads of Faculties. Hence, the library does not come under your administrative control."

Apparently he took up this matter to the Director and Dean, N.S. Venkatesan, (also from Navy), an extremely fair-minded CEO. The Director called us to his office, where Cdr. Gomthi, I and Mr. Desai, my colleague in the library, who had been in the Institute from the day of its inception, were present. While Cdr.Gomti argued on the same lines which he had adopted with me earlier, I cited the *Standing Order*s of the Institute, and also the practice followed all these years. When Cdr.Gomthi continued to twist the argument to suit him, I remember my uttering to him, "Ignorant people should not speak." The matter ended with the Director upholding my stand. The practice of exercising control over the library by the Deputy Dean, the senior most among the Faculties continued. Later, I learnt that Cdr.Gomthi also had a personal interest in helping a direct kin of him, who had just qualified with a degree in library and information science, to get appointed in the library.

Managerial insight : To extend one's area of authority, mere interest- genuine or vested on the part of the power seeker is not sufficient. If an existing chain of command is to be changed, it must be governed by valid reasons, and not just to fulfill the personal interest of an individual. Otherwise, the change is bound to vitiate the working environment, which is not in the interest of the unit, and the larger organization.

8. KNACK OF JUDGING PEOPLE: JUDICIOUS USE OF AUTHORITY

It was the year 2004 when I started writing the book on Knowledge and Information.[1] The book was planned to cover knowledge and its different facets, such as epistemology, information, cognition, intelligence, economics, knowledge management, science and technology, sociology and many other fields. I was sure that the library of the Indian Institute of Management, Bangalore would be of great help to my writing. It was my first meeting with Shri. Chikkamallaiah, the Chief Librarian. After introducing myself, I sought his permission to use the library. He not only gave me the permission to refer, but also the facility of borrowing books and using their excellent databases free of charge. As per their rules, outside parties have to pay for availing loan facilities and accessing their databases, which would work out to a substantial amount. His readily granting that privilege to me, a retired person in his late seventies, meeting him for the first time, and that too having no current institutional affiliation was an enigma to me. I could not desist myself from asking what made him take that decision. I was amazed to hear his explanation. He said that he was present at the Conference on Information held in Bangalore some twenty years ago, where I had presented a paper, which he liked. This, he said was enough for him to conclude that mine is a worthy case to use his authority to relax the rules, and thereby assist the cause of scholarship. Though I felt immensely happy with this, it was always in the back of my mind that I must justify his trust in me by completing the work and see its publication in print.

Managerial insight : Judging people is not easy. It requires an open mind. In exercising one's discretionary powers the manager has to consider the risk involved in the act. It also involves the ability to assess others' integrity, weigh the impact of the decision on the organization, and understanding human psychology on the part of the relaxing authority besides his or her value system.

9. LIMITS OF ONE'S AUTHORITY

This is an incident that occurred while I was serving in IAT. Advance manpower planning is a well established practice in DRDO. Such a plan known as '*Peace Establishment*' (PE), is a document prepared in advance establishing the staff requirements for ten years or so for each establishment in DRDO. Each unit of an establishment prepares the PE based on present activities and future growth of the unit. For IAT, PE plan was worked out based on the new courses to be started, number of students to be admitted, new research projects, the requisite infrastructure, and their financial implications. Plan submitted by each unit is then consolidated to form the PE for the whole establishment. The Library and Information Centre had also submitted its manpower plan. The planned PE for the establishment is then discussed in a meeting presided over by the Chief Controller of Research and Development (CCR&D) representing the DRDO H.Q. Once the proposed PE is approved by the CCR&D it would be submitted to the H.Q. for final sanction.

A meeting chaired by the CCR&D was fixed to discuss and approve the PE. The chairman was a renowned scientist holding a very top position. The staff positions in IAT is made up of two categories: the Wings, mainly dealing with the subject of armaments, weapons, vehicles headed by Directors of Studies; and the Faculties/Departments covering basic and applied sciences headed by civilian scientists. The Directors of Studies presented their plans and it was smooth sailing. Evidently, following their years of training and discipline they had thoroughly vetted their plan documents, probably rehearsed the presentation in advance, and then presented them. It was followed by the presentations by the Heads of faculties, who, it looked, had not done the pre-presentation exercise before presenting their plans. The CCR&D was not pleased with the presentations made by the Heads of Faculties. He started showing his displeasure with the civilian scientists' academic priorities set in their programs. He questioned a professor why his Faculty had taken a particular topic for research, while ignoring other topics (which he had in mind). The professor was an eminent scientist with top class research work to his credit. The Chairman made it clear that he was not satisfied with the explanation given by the professor. If it had ended at that, things would have been smooth. Instead, the Chairman threw a challenging question at the scientists implying "Are you people up-to-date in your subject fields?" Not a single academician in the meeting tried to reply to the question thrown at them. I felt very perturbed about the eminent academicians being thus humiliated collectively. I also felt that the Chairman's assertion should not go unchallenged. In an instant reaction, I stood up and said that I was up-to-date in my subject field. No one had expected this and least the Chairman. It was a real embarrassing moment for him, and evidently he realized it. Then he asked me what was my field; and I replied 'library and information science'. However, he saved the situation for himself by commenting that mine was only an ancillary service field. After the incident a few persons told me that the incident may lead to adverse repercussions on my career. It was the CCR&D's greatness that instead of bearing ill will against me, he and the H.Q. appreciated my work and contributions to the organization. When I think back now, I realize how foolhardy I had been then.

Managerial insight : However high a position one holds in an organization, it does not give him or her the authority to humiliate others. A cardinal feature of good organizational management is to respect human dignity of each individual worker. Quite often such humiliation is tolerated either due to fear of the consequences that may follow from antagonizing the superior authority or the feeling that wisdom lies in treating it as an act of foolishness worth ignoring. The incident also proves how important it is to prepare oneself well in advance and rehearse before presenting a plan or an argument to convince people through effective presentation. Great leaders go by merit of an issue leaving aside personal likes and dislikes. Trying to exercise one's authority beyond a limit is self-defeating.

REFERENCES

1. Narayana, G.J. Knowledge and Information: Perspectives and Prospects. New Delhi, Ess Ess Publicaions, 2010.

5

Libraries and Book-Sellers: E-Publications

Though the basic relationship between libraries and book-sellers is that of a buyer and a seller, it is undergoing a paradigmatic change in recent years. The traditional print form of publication is gradually giving place to e-books, and the printed journal yielding place to online versions. The field is becoming complex with new actors and new issues, such as e-book suppliers (monopolized by Amazon, Flipkart, Landmark and a few others), digital rights mechanism (DRM), and use based subscription instead of outright sale. Libraries are now required to manage more of digital contents, which need a different set of skills and accounting. How libraries, if they survive in their existing or new formats, will cope with the new reality will be known with passage of time. The experiences described below pertain to the print era.

1. BOOK- SELLERS' PART IN COLLECTION BUILDUP

M/s Samarth Subscription Agency, Poona was a one man small book store run by Mr. Pant. Unlike other book stores in the city his shop neither held a large collection of books nor covered a wide range of subjects. The number of customers visiting his store also seemed very limited. Yet his business survived. What was the secret behind that? It was concentrating his efforts mostly to meet the needs of the niche/technical/ institutional segment of users. I had heard a leading bookseller of the city making fun of Mr. Pant with the sneering remark "What! You are purchasing books from such roadside hawkers?" The roadside hawker description fitted Mr. Pant in one particular way. He used to carry the bag filled with books on his shoulders, travel by city bus, and deliver the books on order as well as 'on approval' to the purchasing library, and return back with the unapproved books.

When I took charge of the IAT library, Mr. Pant seemed apprehensive about IAT continuing the purchase of books from him. I could not make out why he entertained such a doubt. One reason could be the thought that the new Head of library might demand rent from him for continuing the purchase. He cannot be entirely faulted for this as there were such instances, though very small in number. When Mr. Pant's apprehension was conveyed to me by Mr. Desai, from whom I took the charge of library, I requested him to assure Mr. Pant not to worry as long as the transactions were fair, open and straight forward. In building IAT library collection, M/s Samarth has played a significant role. The publications supplied by him to IAT were mostly of institutional type and books on highly specialized topics, the procurement of which required special efforts. He was also getting some additional orders by circulating the list of publications supplied by him to IAT library, and thereby reducing his overhead cost per publication. It is book suppliers like him who enabled us to enrich our collection in certain narrow specialized fields to such a standard, and the freedom exercised by library in making selections led to remarks like, "If this book is not in IAT library it is unlikely to be available anywhere else in the country" from users.

Managerial insight : The book-sellers have an important role in the collection build up of libraries. The quality and range of book stock of a library adds to the brand name and reputation of the library. One of the reasons that IAT library built its high reputation for quality service is due to its collection of information resources, particularly its selection and collection of institutional publications, including proceedings of conferences, symposia, standards, and work practices. Keeping track of these types of publications and procuring them in time requires special efforts. Only very few vendors are interested in accepting orders for supplying out-of-the-way publications as it imposes extra efforts, additional expenses and long periods of wait, whereas supplying books on approval may be deemed in some sense as dumping existing stock or newly received publications by the vendor on libraries. Libraries and booksellers have a common stake in the dissemination of knowledge. But this scenario is becoming antiquated.

2. A GAUNTLET THROWN BY A LOCAL BOOK-SELLERS ASSOCIATION

In the supply chain management of libraries, booksellers and publishers constitute a vital link. They have a stake in the development of libraries, especially special and educational libraries. Libraries purchase their books by placing firm orders with book sellers for supply of specific titles and also through 'on approval' basis. Sending latest books to libraries on approval basis was a standard practice followed by many leading book-sellers in the country. On approval basis means that the vendor delivers (mostly) latest publications to a library on a temporary basis for a short period of time to enable the library/ selectors to make the selection by perusal of each publication. The book-seller would collect back the publications that were not selected, and submit the invoices for the ones that were selected and retained by the library. The system worked well and benefited both the parties. As a standard practice the book-sellers allowed 10% 'library discount' on the listed price on all books purchased through 'on approval' basis. The book-sellers were allowed to add 15% handling charges on the listed price in the case of publications that required direct import from abroad on receipt of a firm order.

One day, the Poona (now called Pune) Book-sellers Association took a unilateral decision to discontinue the practice of allowing 10% library discount forthwith. IAT is a major institution in Poona and its purchase of publications was substantial. I was of the view that the decision to withdraw library discount was unreasonable, and also felt that the association should have taken into consideration the views of at least major institutional libraries before imposing that decision. Hence, I refused to accept this. Representatives of the Association visited IAT to present their case before the Deputy Dean and Chairman Library Committee. In the meeting that followed, the association representatives were asked to explain the justification for such a demand. Their main argument was that libraries delayed making payments and took many months to pass the bills, because of which they are forced to borrow money and incur heavy interest out go in order to make payment to the publishers/ distributors in time. The other reason given by them was the long delay in taking decisions by libraries in the case of 'on approval' publications, which results in lost opportunities for the book seller. I challenged them to cite any instance where IAT library had delayed payment (except in cases where there were errors in submitting bills) or delayed in conveying our decisions regarding books delivered 'on approval' to the library. They accepted that IAT was an exception; and they had no complaints against IAT. It was pointed out to them that there was no justification for not allowing 10% discount in the case of IAT as it was very prompt in their dealings with the vendors. However, they said that they could not make an exception of IAT. The book sellers stopped supplying books to IAT.

The gauntlet was accepted. We found a reliable book-seller in Delhi who was willing to supply books with 10% library discount and without adding any transportation charges. The new arrangement worked smoothly. After about four months the local booksellers came back to us and requested to reinstate our association with them, which we did.

Managerial insight : No trade body, and in particular book-sellers, have any justification to throw the gauntlet at their long standing institutional customers, that too without discussing with them in advance; it is not a good marketing strategy. The library authorities must also keep in mind that they are dealing with public money and are accountable as to how it is spent. At the same time, librarians have the onus of maintaining just and fair relationship with their book suppliers. Libraries, the book-sellers and their associations must realize that they have a common stake in promoting the use of books; and they are partners in the cause of promoting the use of knowledge in society. In the new era of e-books and online journals, which has just arrived, the relationship between book vendors and libraries is drastically changing. It will take some time to know what final shape it will take. Library profession must prepare in advance as to how to survive and progress in the changing situation.

3. THREAT OF LEGAL ACTION AGAINST THE LIBRARY

One of the book-sellers supplying books to IAT library one day came to the library and threatened me with initiating legal action against the institute to recover the cost of books supplied, if the same is not paid immediately. I was taken aback by his threat and was worried. I had never come across or heard of an instance of a book supplier filing a case against a library for withholding payment. The fact of the case was that the firm's bills were withheld pending verification of price of the books delivered to the library. As per the terms of supply/prevailing practice, the supplier is to produce price proof when the price is not printed on the publication by producing the publisher's catalogue or the invoice given by the concerned Indian distributor or the foreign agency in case of direct import by the supplier. The library in this case had written a letter to the book-seller to furnish the price proof, which he had not complied with. Hence, I told him that he is free to approach court. When I sought the opinion of a friend, well informed in such matters, his advice was to sort-out the issue amicably. His reason was that any court case will be a prolonged affair, and a private party is better placed to battle out in court than the government.

The book-seller then took up the matter to the Deputy Dean of the Institute. In the meeting with the Deputy Dean I pointed out why the bills are kept pending. He justified our stand and asked the other party to furnish the price proof immediately. It was then that the book-seller came out with the real truth behind his threat. He complained that the library is denying his firm the orders for supply of books and diverting all orders to other firms though his terms of supply are competitive. This was true. Since his service was not up to reasonable professional standards in terms of prompt delivery of ordered publications, correct billing and straightforward correspondence we were forced to reduce drastically placing of orders for books with that firm. He then hinted that the main reason for diverting the orders to other firms is that the librarian is getting rent from other suppliers. This false innuendo against me did not bother me. However, there were strong rumors that a few librarians in the country were deeply involved in such underhand dealings. One black sheep in a large herd is sufficient to tarnish the image of the entire profession.

Managerial insight : Threat is sometimes used as a tactical weapon to get things done in one's favour. Blackmailing may work up to a point when the blackmailed person has something to hide or acted improperly, where discretionary power is used to make illegal gains as quid pro quo. It does not work when the implementing authority knows his job, has no vested interest and of strong character.

6

Discipline

The concept of discipline has two sides: external or physical discipline, and inner or mental discipline. Punctuality, saluting the senior officers by juniors as in the military and police, custom of touching the feet of elders among Hindus, maintaining physical orderliness in space (as in road traffic) are examples for external discipline. The inner/mental discipline is set by sense of justice, moral and professional ethics and human values. Examples for inner discipline include: uprightness of character, professional integrity in conducting research, giving proper acknowledgement of the sources used in publications, performing one's duty without fear or favour. Physical discipline is instilled by practice or regimentation, and threat of punishment. Mental discipline is largely shaped by inheritance, education, and right mentorship, moral and ethical values of a society. Organizational discipline is shaped by the integration of physical and mental discipline of the organizations' stakeholders which determines the culture/ values of the organization. Described below are a few cases of organization related discipline.

1. PUNISHMENT VS. PARDON AS DISCIPLINARY MEASURE

One particular morning, when we entered the IAT campus, it was abuzz with rumors about Mr. Kapale (name changed), the store keeper, being caught red-handed for stealing petrol from the gas station. In the early hours of that morning, covered with a black mask, he was siphoning off petrol from the gas station, using a duplicate key. The theft of petrol was going on for a long time. However, this time he was caught red-handed with the can filled with petrol in his hands by a security guard on patrol duty. He reported the matter immediately to the Chief Administrative Officer (CAO). As per his instructions, Mr.Kapale was detained in the security cell for the night. Mr. Kapale was produced in the morning before Air Cdre. S.K.Nair (AVSM), the Dean of the Institute. All of us expected that he would be suspended forthwith from service, and handed over to the local police lodging a criminal case against him- a normal procedure in such cases. To the surprise of all of us, and to the bewilderment of the CAO, the Dean ordered that Mr.Kapale be removed from his present place of working and posted to a section where there was no scope for committing theft or fraud, and to leave the matter at that. The CAO later told me that when Mr. Kapale was produced before the Dean, he begged for mercy.

Managerial insight : The issue here is applying mercy as a managerial instrument; and whether taking a humanitarian approach is more efficacious than awarding severe punishment, in enhancing discipline in an organization. The possible reasons behind the forgiveness path taken by the Dean could be: a) suspending and putting him behind bars would obliterate any chance of him repenting and reforming; b) any severe punishment, like suspension and dismissal from service would throw the man's family on the streets; c) suspension from service and handing him over to police would involve long administrative and legal procedures that could go on for years without producing any good, in the end, either for the organization or the individual; and d) the assessment that given the nature and quantum of loss caused by the theft, the loss of face and the humiliation suffered by the individual is by itself a just and sufficient punishment. Looking at the incident from this distance of time, it is probable that all these considerations must have weighed with the Dean in arriving at what looks to be the most appropriate, just and honorable decision. Awarding severe punishment would neither have ensured any higher discipline nor would have acted as a deterrent in the long run.

This decision of the dean, in general, had enormous impact on the overall morale of the workers. Later on, in my visit to the home of an employee belonging to Class 4 category of officer (attendant), I found the garlanded photograph of the Dean prominently hung on the wall. The Dean in the photograph was the late Air Cdre. S. K. Nair (AVSM).

2. ABBAS ALI, THE HEAD-STRONG ASSISTANT

One of the first persons to draw my attention in the library after my taking charge as the Head of library at IAT, Poona was Mr. Abbas Ali (name changed), the Library assistant managing the loan counter. I sensed that there seemed to be something seriously wrong with him. Holding the telephone in one hand he was shouting at someone, while a few others were lingering around him. The sight resembled more of a crowded public telephone booth rather than a quiet circulation counter of a library. The library had one telephone and it was at the Counter. Ali exploited this to his advantage. All types of persons were coming to seek his permission to make or receive telephone calls. This not only disturbed the readers, but also affected the work of others. No one in the library wanted to antagonize him because of his rowdy reputation.

One of my first actions after taking control of the library was to shift the telephone from the counter to the librarian's table. This action infuriated Ali as his control over the telephone, which gave him an undeserved personal importance, was removed. In fact, Mr. Desai, the acting librarian who had known me when both of us were in Delhi had already cautioned his colleagues in the library that they would find in the new chief a hard task master, who would not tolerate any casual attitude. Mr. Ali, it seemed, had not heeded to his caution. Instead of becoming sober in his behaviour he started becoming more aggressive. To reach office, I was taking the public transport which had to pass through Kirkee, from where Ali was also taking his bus. He started getting into the same bus by which I was traveling, sit by my side or behind me and start nudging, besides making nasty comments about me. When this went on beyond a limit, I had to take some stern action. I brought this to the notice of the General Staff Officer (GSO-I) and requested him to take immediate disciplinary action against Ali or transfer him from the library. I made it clear that if no immediate action was taken against him, I would take up the matter straight to the dean. Meanwhile, Ali submitted a false complaint against me stating that I was harassing him unnecessarily because of his refusal to do the cooking in my household. Anyone could make out the absurdity of the complaint as Kirkee is about 20 km away from my residence, and me- a pure vegetarian asking a non-vegetarian to come and cook for me. I sent back the complaint with my comments. It was really surprising that Ali did not have the commonsense in cooking up a reason that would look more plausible than that of cooking. He was transferred immediately from the library. It also served as a caution to others that the new Head would not allow any indiscipline in the library.

Managerial insight : In matters of indiscipline taking timely corrective action prevents the situation from getting worse. Such an action also serves as a caution for others in the Section/ Department that indiscipline will not be tolerated irrespective of the person involved.

3. IS INCORRIGIBLENESS IRREVERSIBLE?

No! It is reversible, as can be seen from the following case. Mr. Swaraj Gupthe (name changed) was working as an attendant in the library of ADE for the past several years. His habit of dodging work was well known. His frequent absence from the work place always proved a problem for the supervisory staff. He could not be transferred to any other department in the establishment as no unit would welcome him. A well noticed feature about him was his attitude, "come what may, I don't care". To express in one word he was incorrigible. The problem of managing this incorrigibleness confronted me at the very beginning of my joining ADE. An analysis of the situation showed that he was intelligent; could work hard and had the drive to excel, if he wanted to. Since he was allowed to remain obdurate for so long, 'care not' attitude became his nature. What he needed was proper guidance and firmness in dealing with him. To bring about a transformation in his work behaviour, the first step needed was to create in him the feeling of trust in me that my dealings with him would be honest and fair. The officer under whom he was working had complained to me several times on Swaraj's indiscipline and disobedience, which fact, I was sure, Swaraj was aware of. Since I had come to know that the two had fallen out over some money lending transactions, thus vitiating the complaint, I had not acted upon those complaints. It so happened that on one occasion, I had to reprimand the officer publicly for his shirking of responsibility. This and the fact that I had ignored the officer's complaints against Swaraj must have given him the feeling of trust in me.

One day some 15 minutes before lunch time, the officer came to me in an agitated mood and complained that Swaraj was disobeying his orders to shift books to the next room. Accompanied by the officer, I confronted Mr. Swaraj and asked whether it was true that the officer had instructed him to shift the books, and he refused to carry out his instruction. He responded by saying that he told the officer that it was nearing lunch time, and he would shift the books after the lunch break. He was reluctant to carry out the work immediately. I told him firmly that it was not proper on his part to behave like that. I also ordered him to abide by the instruction by immediately shifting at least one or two bundles, as a token of obedience. I also volunteered to assist him by myself carrying a few bundles, if he wanted to. After thinking for a minute or two, he began complying with my instructions. That was the turning point in his behaviour. Since then I never heard a complaint against him from any quarters. This also resulted in a good personal rapport between us, which I value even today.

Managerial insight : Incorrigibleness is not irreversible. It takes proper guidance from the leader or the immediate line manger to bring the change. Mutual trust between the leader and the fellow workers is a key factor in bringing the desired behavioural changes in the persons entrusted to the manager's charge.

4. MY PROBLEM GETS SOLVED WITHOUT MY EFFORTS

Mr. Krishnan (name changed), on his joining as Junior Scientific Officer at INSDOC, was posted to my section. I was happy that we would work together, as we happened to be classmates and friends at one time. Before his joining, he had sought my opinion about the INSDOC offer. I had expressed my view that it was an excellent offer, and he must accept it. When he came to Delhi to join duty he requested me to allow him and his wife to stay at my place for a few days until he could rent a suitable house. They stayed with me for over a month. My happiness about this arrangement did not last long. The main problem was about his unpunctual attendance. From day one he was coming late to the section by 30 minutes to 45 minutes. It was an embarrassing situation to handle. First, I tried indirect ways like waiting for my friend to arrive and then asking a colleague, in a loud voice, the time or discussing on the virtues of punctual attendance so that on hearing it my friend would grasp its significance. It didn't work. Hence, I had to tell him directly that his coming late every day was not acceptable to me. To my shock, he questioned me how I could say he was late when neither there was a clock in the room nor I had a watch to fix the time of his arrival. I kept quiet. The same evening I bought a wrist watch for the first time in my life. As usual, when Krishnan arrived late the next day, I showed him the time in my watch, which confirmed his late arrival. With red face he went out of the Section and returned after some time. The next morning I received an order stating that Mr. Krishnan was transferred from my section, and a substitute posted in his place. Evidently, the previous day when he went out, he had met the Director and had complained against me.

Managerial insight : When it comes to work culture, organizational interest must precede personal interests and relationships. Enforcing even reasonable discipline often leads to embitterment of relationship between the involved parties, but one has to face it. Allowing continued indiscipline, including unpunctual attendance, on the part of even one employee will affect the morale of the whole unit. Unrestrained, continued indiscipline is bound to become a habitual behaviour of the person, which will be difficult to rectify later.

5. THE TALE AAROUND A NOISY SHOE

It is a well known fact that noise pollutes environment and is to be avoided in public places. It is more so in libraries where noise disturbs readers and reading. This case of noise related indiscipline occurred while I was serving as Documentation Officer in the Publications and Information Directorate (PID), a unit of the CSIR, New Delhi. Miss. Zenith (name changed) joined my unit as a Technical Assistant on transfer from another CSIR Laboratory. A disturbing factor about her was her shoes. Every time she walked, her shoes made such a loud harsh noise, it was unbearable to others. Without heeding my requests and advice, she continued with her acoustic nuisance. As a last resort, I had to threaten her with initiating disciplinary action against her. She changed her footwear, thereby ending the noise disturbance. But the incident did not end there. It was rumored that Miss Zenith had a powerful godfather in the CSIR HQ., and it was due to his influence that she had landed in PID. The rumor turned out to be true. About a month after this incident, I was advised in confidence by a reliable source that I should be careful as a scheme was being worked out under the guidance of her godfather to teach me a lesson. It was apparent that she had complained against me to her godfather. A couple of months later, when I met her godfather on a courtesy call before my exit from CSIR, it became clear from his talk that indeed I was on his radar.

Managerial insight : Every environment demands our adherence to the discipline governing that environment. Not following the decorum binding a given environment is mostly due to one's insensitiveness to others' feelings or ignorance or imperiousness. In most cases a request or advice will be sufficient to solve this problem. When request or advice does not work, it needs to be treated as a case of gross indiscipline.

6. BOOK-SHELF PLANK AS FOOT-REST

While searching for books in a library, the habit of resting one's foot on the bottom plank of a book-shelf is not uncommon, but is limited to a miniscule of users of libraries. This habit always annoyed me. For me it was a question of maintaining decorum. For people who think that a library is a temple of learning, and a book is an incarnation of goddess Saraswathi, this habit is intolerable. When display of such habits occurred (quite a few times) it was a piquant situation for the lower level staff members in the library to point this out, if the persons involved were of officer's rank. Invariably, it fell upon me to request the concerned party to desist from the bad habit. It is to the credit of the officers that they would see their mistake and rectify it.

Managerial insight : Every organization establishes and maintains certain values, rules and practices. It expects its stakeholders to honour them. Sometimes due to involuntary habit or ignorance, one may fail to adhere to the norm. In most such instances, a polite reminder to follow the norms will solve the problem. Where the set rules/practices are of particular importance to the unit, it is essential to bring them to the notice of the users through prominent display.

7. A CHALLENGING DIVISION TO MANAGE

The reprographic section in ADE, consisting of design, drawing, printing and copying sections was known for its indiscipline. No officer wanted to handle that section. Just after four months of my taking charge of the library, the Director wanted me to take charge of that section as an additional assignment. Quite a few workers in that section were behaving like lords, as if they were above the rule of law. Indiscipline was rampant; evading work was common; corruption in the purchase of paper, ink and other stationery items also existed. Narrated here are two typical accounts.

(a) Drunkenness in Workplace : One morning on a casual visit to the section, I found that one of the workers was in a fully inebriated condition. I later learnt that it was not a lone case. It was also rumored that one of the workers was even selling liquor openly in the section. It was a new experience for me to tackle this situation. When I took up this issue with the Chief Administrative Officer (CAO), he asked me to file a complaint in writing so that he would initiate disciplinary action against the concerned individual. I then consulted a colleague officer whose approach to administrative issues was always pragmatic. His advice was not to lodge the complaint, but tackle the issue in a tactical manner. The reasons he gave were quite straightforward. For initiating any disciplinary action against the person, first it is to be proved that he is drunk at the time of reporting. To prove this, the person should be produced before a government doctor, who has to conduct his breath analysis, based on which he must confirm that the person is drunk. Even if he gives a positive report, the establishment will suspend him and then constitute a court of enquiry (COE) to establish his guilt. Before the COE you are the accuser and he is the accused, but both are treated as equals. It is for you to produce the evidences to establish his guilt, whereas the accused has only to defend. It is more likely that his friendly colleagues as witnesses will stand by him, and not you. It is possible that the COE concludes that he is guilty and even recommends for termination of his service. If his service is terminated, he is sure to approach a court of law. The case will prolong for years, and if the judgment comes out in his favour, he then comes back with a bloated head and mocks at you and the establishment. So, my friend said, "you decide whether you want to put yourself in that position." The course of action was clear.

I called the person when he had become sober and also two reliable workers from the Reprographic section to my office. I told the person that a complaint of drunkenness against him was ready and I would file it immediately. This being his first offence, I was offering him a chance to come out of the bad situation, but under one condition. The condition was that he must apologize in writing accepting his bad conduct, with the promise that he would not repeat it again. He not only gave his apology in writing, but also kept to his promise.

Managerial insight : Severe disciplinary action is called for only in cases of serious offences. Initiating any disciplinary action, other than giving a warning, is cumbersome and time consuming. The worst thing about disciplinary action is that before the judging authority the culprit and the complainant stand at par. The onus of proving that the person has committed the offence is on the complainant- a more difficult, cumbersome and time consuming affair. It is easier to defend than establishing the offence. Hence, it is always preferable to adopt other means such as counselling and threat of disciplinary action to get the desired results. Initiating severe disciplinary action such as suspension from service should be used as the last option, when all other means fail.

(b) A Printer Trying to Hoodwink the Divisional Head : One of the annual routine assignments of the reprographic section of ADE was to produce the New Year Greeting Cards for the establishment. Though the design of the card was given to the printing section well in advance, invariably the section used to drag on the work till the last day of December or early January. This left little time for dispatching the greeting cards. It had gone on like this for many years. Mr. Prakash (name changed), the printer responsible for bringing out the cards, always used this recurring assignment as a strategy to show his importance and indispensability to the section. I had taken charge of the section two months earlier, and the beginning of the New Year was only two weeks away. This time too he tried to play the same game with me. He came out with all sorts of unreasonable demands, such as sanctioning overtime for a week for him and his co-workers; purchase of fresh stationery, even though enough materials were in stock; arrangement of tea and snacks during the hours of overtime. Even after agreeing to his demands, he would not commit to complete the job within the given target date. It was a serious challenge thrown at me. Given the fact that it was my first year of service in the establishment, my managerial ability was at stake. After a meeting with two of the reliable printing assistants and the art designer, I entrusted the work to them. They were asked to complete the printing job without the help of Mr. Prakash. I assured them of all the help they needed to deliver the cards before the end of third week of December. Mr. Prakash was sternly told that he was debarred from entering the section till the printing work was completed. This had the desired effect on Mr.Prakash, and he fell in line. Meanwhile, I had kept ready an alternate plan of getting the cards printed from outside at my personal expense, in case of contingency. The New Year Greeting cards were printed and delivered well ahead of time for the first time in many years.

I also found out that Mr. Prakash was indulging in fraud in the purchase of stationery items for the printing section. He had put up for my approval a number of bills in which the items were heavily over priced. The purchase rule required that the order should be placed on the firm quoting the lowest bid among three competitive quotations. Mr. Prakash evidently in connivance with select firms had obtained the quotations with manipulated prices. Through reliable persons, I obtained fresh quotations for the same items from firms excluding the firms selected by Prakash. It was found that the rates were almost 40% lower than the ones put-up by Prakash. I confronted him with these facts and asked for explanation for producing fraudulent bills. He had no satisfactory explanation, and at last he came out with the truth. Since he accepted his folly and repented, the issue was closed on his apologizing in writing.

Managerial insight : The dysfunction of the section was primarily due to: a) lack of proper control over workers over a period of years, b) faulty organization structure of the division in terms of span of control; c) neglect to insist on functional accountability and performance audit, and d) lack of motivation.

7

Quality Maintenance: Brand Building

When a product or a service that is not the monopoly of a single manufacturer or a service provider, then the customers have a choice in buying that product or procuring that service. This leads to a competitive situation where the user/customer can exercise choice. One of the critical factors that go to influence the customer in making her or his choice to buy is the quality aspect of the service rendered or the brand name associated with the product on sale. In the market economy and consumer world the manufacturers of products and providers of services use the concept of brand names and brand building to associate the quality of the product or service in the minds of customers. Because of the nature of library and information services brand names and brand building as conceived in trade and industry cannot be strictly applied. But the essence of brand building is very much relevant to libraries and information services, and takes the form of creating reputation in the minds of the users, about the library and its services, in terms of quality.

A service based on excellence/goodness adds to the reputation of the library. While constantly trying to improve upon the library service to higher standards of excellence, one must not get bogged down to achieve perfection. By pursuing excellence as a fad one is unlikely to achieve anything. In this context, it is pertinent to bear in mind that "Best is the enemy of the good"- one of the basic principles of library and information science postulated by Donald Urquhart.[1] Quality maintenance is a prime factor that goes to enhance the reputation of a library in the minds of its users and the community. Quality is one of the key elements that go to make a 'best practice'.

1. BRAND NAMES AND BRAND BUILDING

Brand equity, also known also known as brand value, implies that consumers prefer to buy a product with well known name than a product with less well known name. Thus a branded product increases sale and brings more money to manufacturer (Wikipedia 2012).

The concept of brand name and the process of brand building are highly valued and widely used in industry and commerce. The essence of brand building is to create positive image in the minds of customers towards a particular product or service. It is to influence the customer to buy the particular branded item in preference to other competing brands. Often the marketing strategy of a company, especially its advertising plan is built around its brand name. Larger the enterprise and higher the competition, greater is the money budgeted for brand building and advertising. Commercial and industrial enterprises consider brand value as an intangible asset which can be monetized.

A brand is a name, a slogan, a logo or a combination of them selected to serve as the most effective communication bridge between the business enterprise/products and the consumer- existing and potential. A brand is associated with quality and value for money in the minds of customers. A brand is also a measure of the trust it commands among the consumers. If the marketing strategy towards the existing customers is to retain their continued loyalty and build upon it, the issue with the potential consumers is that of influencing them to become actual customers. Even in the domain of business and industry, it is large enterprises and companies with a number of retail outlets that are most conscious of the importance of brand equity in promoting business and carving out niche position in their respective markets.

Though brand building has an important role to play in promoting not- for- profit organizations and services, it is not fully exploited by them. Since brand building is largely associated with trade and industry, one may have reservations about its relevance to libraries. This need not be so. What is needed is innovative approach. Library managers seem to have not given sufficient thought to brand building. Brand building in marketing consists of: a) creation of the brand, i.e. deciding what or which aspects of the product should be highlighted, which in the case of a library corresponds to the aspects of library that needs to be highlighted, so that the user is attracted to use the library, b) packaging, which in the case of library refers to the library timings, location of library to meet the convenience of the user population, c) advertising the brand, i.e. indicating the variety and depth of collection, and mode of delivery of the library service; and d) selling the brand to user population. Libraries are yet to fully exploit the e-media, particularly the social media like facebook in publicizing its brand name, besides traditional means like visual display, bringing library-community contacts, use of press media and the like.

For library and information centre sector, building brand image may not be easy or possible due to its several constraining features. The major constraining features of libraries are: a) they are not-for-profit organizations, b) they survive in a noncompetitive world, though the situation has changed with the arrival of online publications, c) organizationally they exist as parts of a larger organization (exception being public library systems supported by the state), such as schools, colleges, higher institutions of learning; academic institutions, R&D organizations, and government departments, d) they are service organizations, and e) their survival does not depend on marketing. Yet, when the concept of brand equity takes the form of trust/reputation building, it is very much relevant to libraries and information centres. Here, trust stands for the perception and experience of the users about the efficiency and effectiveness of the service provided. Efficiency is mainly concerned with saving of time and labour, where as effectiveness is a measure of the service providers' approach to users, knowing their needs and their actual fulfillment in a cordial atmosphere. To gain the trust of the users a library has to work on two fronts- a) reactive, i.e. meeting the current expressed needs of users, and b) proactive, i.e. anticipating the requirements of clients in advance and taking steps to fulfill them. The factors that go to make or mar the reputation of a library are: the quality of service rendered, ease of access to information resources, extent of fulfillment of needs of users, and dependability of service. Described below are examples of library brand building and a few of its features:

Managerial insight : Brand name and brand building are marketing concepts fully exploited by industry and commerce. A brand is associated with quality and value for money in the minds of customers. It is to help retain existing customers and attract new customers. By creating a library brand value in the minds of users a library can serve its readers more effectively and also increase its users.

2. IAT INFORMATION CENTRE AND LIBRARY : BRAND BUILDING

The function of brand building in business enterprises mostly falls under the marketing department. Public Relations department also plays a role in brand building. However, in building the reputation of a library, every staff member of the library plays a part by working as a team. It is for the manager/ Chief Librarian to motivate them and ensure each member of the team tries individually and collectively to enhance the value of the library to its users. The reputation is built or gets enhanced when the community of users really feels that the library has contributed significantly in its progress towards obtaining the requisite information to help attain their goals. The fact that the information support given by the Library and Information Center (IC&L) of the IAT, Poona finds a mention in the acknowledgment part of research papers published by many of the scientists and scholars of the Institute is a testimony to its high reputation. Its high brand value could be gauged from the fact that a visit to IC&L invariably found a place in the agenda of VIPs visiting the Institute. This included Mr. Chou en Lai, the Chinese prime minister.

Public relations : Building and maintaining good public relations with the stake holders and the community of users is a part of modern day public life- whether it is political, professional, industrial or business. Many organizations and industrial enterprises maintain separate Public relations department headed by a Public relations officer (PRO). Libraries cannot afford to appoint PROs due to the constraints listed earlier; and at the same time PR functions cannot be ignored. What libraries can do is to train one of its staff members, preferably the one who is in greater contact with the user community, like the Reference librarian or Circulation-in-charge and entrust PR work as an additional assignment. PR functions include promoting cordial relationship with the stake holders and making them aware of the services of the library, and getting the feed back from them to improve its services. Good and effective PR will help create enormous goodwill towards the library in the minds of its stake holders and the community. This in itself is a great source of strength to the library in its further development. Mere PR work unless backed by effective and efficient service by the library results only in superficial admiration by the users.

For student officers passing out annually from IAT, and to most readers of IAT, the library meant "Raghu" (the late R. Raghu Raman) and "Desai" (H.G. Desai). So was Shri K. Venkatesh of the Institute for Social and Economic Studies in Bengaluru. These were the staff members of the libraries, who with their excellent knowledge of library resources and its intellectual contents, and personal commitment to help the users represented the image of their libraries, respectively; and fulfilled partially the brand building function for the library. With their knack to establish fruitful relationships with external agencies they were also fulfilling a public relations function (PR) for the library, without calling it as such. They were successful in discharging the PR part, other than the press/media contact and visual publicity part, as they had the requisite personal qualities and communication skills. In ADE library the function of brand building and PR work was largely fulfilled by Mr. M. N. Nadgir,

Mrs. Pramila Chabria, and in later years by Mrs. S. H. Leelavathi, who also received DRDO Day Award for the year 2010 for her excellent contributions. What they needed was the opportunity and the necessary exposure, provision of which was the responsibility of the Head of Library. It is this category of persons who form the brand ambassadors of a library/ information centre.

Managerial insight : Though every staff member of a library has a role to play in building the brand value, it is the service staff and the top manager of the library who make or mar the brand name. The brand value is built or gets enhanced when the community of library users honestly feels and acknowledges that the library has contributed significantly in their pursuits. PR functions of a library include promoting cordial relationship with the stake holders and making them aware of the services of the library, and getting the feed back from them to improve its services. Mere PR work cannot be a substitute for effective, efficient and dedicated service by the library.

3. ONE UNIT'S DEFAULT MAY BE ANOTHER UNIT'S GAIN

One late morning Col. Bikram Singh (name changed) of the Army Wing of IAT came to the IC&L looking for a particular technical report. One could read frustration etched on his face. He approached the Reference assistant to find out whether the library had that report. The catalogue showed that the library had it. Since the report was not in the stack, the assistant after checking the loan records informed Col.Singh that the library has that report, it had been lent out, and the name of the person to whom it was lent, and when it was due for return. It was a great mental relief to Col. Singh. The background for that relief was that before coming to library he had been to three different departments to check about certain cases pertaining to his Wing. In all the three units he got very vague or negative replies, which was of no help to him. This generated a feeling of frustration in him. In contrast to this, his experience with the library was one of relief and satisfaction. We were happy to hear him utter to himself words to the effect, "there is at least one unit in the Institute which works efficiently, and knows what it is doing."

Managerial insight : In an organizational setup, sometimes one unit gets credit not entirely because of its own making, but because of the default on the part of other units in the system. In this case, the library did not do anything extraordinary to get that appreciation, but discharged the functions expected from it. It is the default of other units that elevated the standing of the library in Col. Singh's perception. This can be psychologically explained in terms of general human reaction to fulfillment of a want against the repeat experience of frustration caused by belied expectations. In contrast is the situation where a defaulting unit to cover-up its lapses makes another unit/person a scapegoat. (See 3.9).

4. A GENUINE APPRECIATION OF LIBRARY SERVICE

Over telephone Col. Ranganathan, Head of Guided Weapons Wing of IAT requested the presence of me and my colleague H.G. Desai at the Wing's assembly line at 0900 hours next day morning. This call from the Colonel surprised us. We pondered over the possible reason for his asking us to be there. I thought probably he wanted to discuss some matter about the information service. He was a person deeply involved in his work, and a 'no nonsense' type of officer. Hence, a call from him meant that something serious was the matter. At that time he was working on a project on developing a prototype retro-rocket.

When we reached the place, there were some twenty persons giving final touches to an engine. We could feel a sense of excitement in the group. Col. Ranganathan welcomed us and pointed at the engine. He said that it was a momentous event to see the culmination of his team's nearly eight years of sustained labour. He had set that morning as the time for the final trial of the rocket developed by them. He wanted to share his joy with us. Then he pressed the control switch and the rocket fired as per the design. It was a grand success. All those present were overjoyed. Then, he showed us the rocket and explained its working. For me, the reason for his inviting us from the library still remained a puzzle. A few minutes later, when he thanked us for the help he received from the library, the reason became clear.

It took me to an event that occurred nearly four years earlier. One morning, Col. Ranganathan came to me in a highly distressed mood. Anxiety was writ large over his face. He asked me whether the library could help him in solving a major technical problem. He was stuck with a serious technical snag at a crucial stage in the development of the retro-rocket. He also told me that he had checked with all the available literature and consulted other specialists and establishments working in the field of rocketry and aeronautics in the country without success. At that time the technology of retro-rocket was known only to the Americans, the British and the Germans, who kept it as a highly guarded secret. He had got into an apparently insurmountable situation forcing him to decide whether to go ahead with the project or abandon it. I took him to Mr. Desai, my colleague, who was well versed with the literature of the field. The Colonel explained the problem to him. Desai, after searching through several racks in the books, journals, conference proceedings and classified reports sections, picked up a publication. After going through the contents, he spotted a page containing a complicated design and asked the Colonel whether that was the problem he was referring to. The Colonel spent a long time going through the text and then gave an excited cry. There in the text was the solution to his problem. Clutching the volume he left in a highly jubilant mood. In the moment of his glory, he remembered that event, and told us how it helped him to proceed with the project and see its successful completion. For us it was a rare and genuine appreciation of our work. Though I have received a few awards and appreciations in my career, including 'the Scientist of the Year' award bestowed by Mrs. Indira Gandhi, the Hon. former Prime Minister of the country; this appreciation from the user is of special significance to me.

Managerial insight : Showing appreciation of a service rendered or work completed is common. Of course, there are persons for whom appreciating good work or achievement of others and expressing it is something to be avoided, not necessarily due to prejudice. For some persons, expressing appreciation is a formality, for many others it is bait used to get the work done; but a genuine appreciation is not that common and is of rare value. It is such appreciations that reflect the quality of service rendered by a good library and information centre, which enhances its brand name. A genuine appreciation is a great motivator.

5. APPRECIATION OF SERVICE BY VIPS AND SECONDARY USERS

Any useful and quality contribution made towards increasing the use of information service by the community of users for whom it exists and also by other external users does not go unrecognized. Two such appreciations, representative of several others received from external users on the services provided by the IC&L of IAT are reproduced here:

(i) Vivek R.Sinha, Chief Controller Research & Development, Department of Defence R&D, Ministry of Defence, Sena Bhavan, New Delhi 110011, vide D.O. letter dated 22 May 1982:

"..... During my recent visit to IAT, Pune, I was highly impressed by the scientific manner in which the Library is being run. Please convey my appreciation to all officers/ staff who are engaged in providing useful service to the teaching staff as well as students through the Library."

(ii) Brig Gurbir Mansingh, DDWE (Op Requirements), Weapons & Equipment Directorate, General Staff Branch, Army Headquarters, New Delhi-110001, vide letter dated 29th April 82:

"....We were very happy to receive a copy of your publication "WEAPONS LITERATURE FROM PERIODICALS: 1970-1981", which will be very useful to us here. I see from your introductory note that separate publications have been issued covering armour and missiles and rockets (other than battlefield). If you have a separate copy of each available, I would be very grateful if you could send me one of each.

May I take this opportunity of complementing all concerned on the involved work needed to bring such a useful publication."

Quite often, an information product produced to meet

the requirements of a particular user group is also found useful to others dealing with the same or closely connected topics. A multiple use/user product can be distributed without additional cost, other than the cost of providing access, and thereby multiply the returns on the resources invested on the production of information as in b) above.

Managerial insight : For any work, information product or service to be recognized by the user community, it has to be useful to them or meet an unfulfilled need, and it must adhere to certain quality standard. Generally, such works/projects are the outcome of team work. The selection of project, meeting an unmet demand, and recognizing an existing opportunity to create a useful product or service requires an innovative mind and vision on the part of the leader/manager. The appreciation received not only brings immense satisfaction to the members of the team, and acts as a motivator, but also justifies the efforts put in to produce the good. Earning of such recognition enhances the reputation/ brand value of the organization/unit and helps its further growth.

6. TRUST IN THE LIBRARY'S ABILITY TO DELIVER SERVICE

One day, while serving in ARDE, Bangalore, I received an unexpected telephone call from the Director of ARDE, Poona (a sister establishment of IAT, Poona). He wanted the name of the British biologist who had settled in India and information about him. It so happened that I had read about J.B.S. Haldane and so I could immediately give the name, and requested him to give me a few minutes to furnish full details on J.B.S. Haldane. He told me that he was in Bangalore to deliver a speech/attend a meeting. This incident took place after I had left IAT, Poona and had joined the ADE, Bangalore.

He further added that he wanted the information quickly and, he was sure in his mind, that he would get it by approaching me. The background of the Director's confidence in me seemed to be that when I was in IAT, he had known my work and was aware of the quality and reliability of the service provided by IAT library. He was also aware of our using the information resources and facilities of his organization to provide enhanced benefit to the larger community of users, including ARDE. I was gratified at his remembering me, and associating my name with providing prompt and reliable information. I did not belie his trust in my ability to deliver the requisite information, even after so many years from my exit from IAT, Poona. It was an invaluable complement, in which the brand value of the organizational unit as well as the reputation of the individual actor has combined together.

Managerial insight : There was nothing extraordinary about the reference service provided in this case. What is worth noting here is the supreme trust the Director had in me and in my ability to fulfill his information need, even though I had left IAT, Pune longtime back. It is the reputation/brand name of the IAT library for providing quality service etched in the minds of users coupled with the trust in the ability of the concerned professional that makes the incident remarkable.

7. APPLICATION OF MIND

One day one of the scientists of ADE came to me with the request for making an exhaustive literature search on an engineering topic. I requested my junior colleague Mr. Sheshadri (name changed) to conduct a literature search on the topic with the suggestion that he might begin the search with *The Engineering Index.* After a day I asked him how was he progressing with the search?. To my shock he told me that there was no article on the subject in *The Engineering Index.* I could not believe it. Then I spent some time searching in the *Engineering index.* I could identify about 20 items on the topic.. I showed him the items and asked him how he could miss them. To make sure that the items that I had located were on the specified topic and are relevant, took Mr. Sheshadri with me, and went to check with the concerned scientist. He was given the list and the two Index volumes from where some six of the selected items were marked, to get their subject matter confirmed. After scanning the list and studying the items in the Index volumes he confirmed that the items are relevant and wanted. After this, my colleague started the literature search again, compiled a useful and more comprehensive list of references on the topic and passé it on to the concerned scientist.

What I could not make out was how and why my colleague

failed to identify the items at the first instance. There was no reason for him to fail to locate even a single item, given his subject background, experience, intelligence and the position he was holding. If he was unable to understand the topic at least in broad terms- a prerequisite for beginning the search, he could have consulted a subject specialist or relevant reference publications to grasp what the topic stood for. Probably it is a case of lack of application of mind on his part or a disturbed state of mind.

Managerial insight : Proper application of mind to the given task is an essential requirement in completing the task to full satisfaction. One may be intelligent, creative and experienced, yet unless there is application of mind, he or she cannot achieve much. One or two occurrences like this, even if unintentional, are sufficient to mar the reputation of the library for rendering quality service in the minds of library users, and a cause of concern for top management.

REFERENCES

1. Urquhart, Donald. Principles of Librarianship. Bardsey, Wood Garth, 1981.

8

Educational Functions of Libraries

The role of libraries in transfer of knowledge and providing information is well known. The educational function of libraries has not received much attention in the profession. Whatever educational function is discharged is mostly limited to reader education, i.e., acquainting readers with the use of library, and familiarizing readers with different sources of information like encyclopedias, reports, patents and so on. Now it includes educating the users in the use of Internet dependent services and multimedia resources. Educational function of libraries goes beyond this. Occasionally it may include mentoring. A few of the instances involving educational function encountered by the author are narrated here.

1. LIBRARIAN'S ROLE IN THE SELECTION OF TEXTBOOKS

As noted earlier, the IAT is a higher institute of military technology and defence related R&D. It runs a number of courses both of short term and long term duration. Hence, the textbook collection plays a vital part in the educational activities of the Institute. The library had built up a good textbook collection. At this juncture of time Maj. Gen. N. Subba Rao (AVSM) came as the Director and Dean of the Institute. Long time back, he had a tenure in the Institute as Superintendent of Workshop and teaching workshop technology to the courses.

On his first visit to the library he spent some time in the textbooks section going through various titles, particularly relating to workshop technology. He took out two titles and asked me why the two books, which were very outdated, were still being used, particularly when new titles covering the latest developments were available. Annoyed at his putting that question to me, I pointed out that prescribing textbooks is the responsibility of the faculty members, and not that of the library. The role of the library is limited to procurement of prescribed textbooks and making them available to students. In a very calm, but firm tone he explained to me that a librarian who lives in the world of books is in an excellent position to know the books that are relevant and current to the requirements of teaching, as book world is his special domain. It is a part of the educational function of the library to bring to the notice of the faculty the weakness in the collection, if any. If he does not do it, he is failing in his professional duties. It was the first time in my career that some one had pointed out my shortcoming. Though the library actively participated in the selection of books and collection buildup, I had failed to bring textbooks into the fold of collection buildup. I accepted my lapse in this regard and genuinely apologized. I was beginning to feel ashamed of myself. It was his greatness that he grasped my feelings, and tried to reassure me by saying that such things happen sometimes in everybody's career, but one must take a wider perspective of his work domain.

Managerial insight : A librarian's professional functions, especially in educational institutions, have an educational dimension, which needs to be recognized and fulfilled. The educational function takes different forms, such as active role in the selection of books and effective collection buildup, guidance to readers in the use of library collection, conducting short term seminars and courses on topics relevant to the community of users and the like. It is human to err, but greatness lies in accepting one's error and overcoming it. Real leaders know the art of pointing out the drawbacks of an employee and create awareness in him or her without giving rise to rancour. One is reminded of the proverb "to err is human, to forgive is divine."

2. COURSE ON DEFENCE SCIENCE INFORMATION

IC&L of IAT always tried to fulfill its library and information functions effectively and efficiently. However, the incidence relating to textbooks selection narrated earlier prompted me to think further on the educational function of a library in an institution like IAT. After careful thinking and discussions with select faculty members it was felt that there was a need for conducting an appreciation course on "Information Handling for Defence R&D" for DRDO scientists, engineers and technologists . It took the form of a 10 day Course conducted from 14 to 24th December, 1982. The course was designed in two parts: Part-I dealing with the role of library and information in increasing R&D productivity, and Part-II covering the disciplines constituting defence science and technology and their applications. The objective of the course was two-fold: a) to make senior level scientists, engineers and managers of DRDO establishments aware of the problems of information handling and maximizing information use; and b) to present them with the state of the art exposition of different disciplines with which DRDO is concerned, thereby serving as a platform for transfer and sharing of relevant knowledge. While designing the course, it was kept in mind that the DRDO recruited a large number of fresh graduate apprentices, who would become future leaders guiding the future destiny of DRDO. The course would help senior scientists and technologists in guiding the apprentices.

An outstanding feature of the course were the two inspiring general lectures delivered by Dr. R.G. Takwale, the Vice Chancellor, University of Poona on the implications of information revolution for higher education— the central theme of his inaugural address; and the lecture delivered by the late Shri. N. M. Ketkar, the former Director of National Social Science Documentation Centre, New Delhi on 'Knowledge and its role in R&D'. The course was a success beyond our expectations.

The most disappointing part of this educational initiative of IAT library was that the course could not be conducted in the subsequent year due to the strong opposition raised at the H.Q. by a sister central establishment insisting that it was their right to conduct such courses. However, in private they acknowledged the need for such a course and recognized the high quality and relevance of the course conducted by IC&L of IAT. The pity was that those who opposed IAT library conducting the course had neither the vision nor the organizing ability to conduct such courses, nor the tolerance to others conducting them. It reminds me of the "dog in the manger" policy.

To the best of my knowledge, it was for the first time in the country that a library organized a senior level course for the scientific and engineering community of a multidisciplinary organization, encompassing topics on information, use of library resources, and the developments in the major scientific and technical fields covered by the different establishments and laboratories of DRDO. The resource persons for the course were drawn from the faculties and Wings of IAT, other sister establishments, and outside for covering different disciplines constituting military technology, and IAT library and outside experts for covering information part of the course. Apart from the lectures, the course included visits to Bhabha Atomic Research Centre (BARC), and the Indian Institute of Technology (IIT), Bombay. It was very satisfying for us to learn that the course was highly successful in achieving the set objectives. This was evident from the feedback received from the participants, who rated the usefulness of the course and the manner in which it was conducted as very high. The participants were unanimous that the course should become an annual feature. We in the library were extremely happy that we justified the confidence Brig.G. Ramalingam, the then Officiating Director and Dean of the Institute had in the relevance and usefulness of the course, and in our ability to successfully organize such a course.

Managerial insight : To survive and progress, organizations need to be innovative. Libraries are no exception to this. Of course, the opportunities for innovations in the library and information field are not very large and varied as in industry, trade and commerce. Any innovative initiative taken by a library that improves its service or brings in value addition is always welcomed by the user community. Innovation need not be limited to the main library functions or library technology application; it can be extended to new but not hitherto thought out areas like educational function of libraries, novel opportunities in the social, cultural and community functions of libraries. To create one good thing, surely there will be several hindrances; but the joy lies in achieving the goal against all odds, especially caused by jealousy, ego and sometimes inter-institutional rivalry. Innovativeness is one of the criteria that can be used to distinguish one library from another.

9
Language Skills

Communication is the vehicle through which relationships are established, promoted or broken. Language is the prime means of communication in societies, organizations and institutions. Language and thinking are closely interrelated, thus giving rise to the saying "think before you ink." In career and personal life how we use language in conducting transactions or establishing effective communication can make or mar success. Choice of vocabulary and mode of delivery of spoken and written word are two important aspects of using language effectively. Effective use of language is possible only when there is proper coordination between semantics, syntax and psychology of communication created by the selection of words used, the context of use, the tone and the body language of the parties to the communication. Language also has an emotional facet, which causes division or cohesion in society. What follows are a few aspects of language use and language related experiences.

1. PROBLEM CAUSED BY LIMITED EXPOSURE TO LANGUAGE

The following incident shows how the limited proficiency in language almost blocked a job opportunity.

It was my first interview. The venue was North Block Secretariat, the institution was the Central Secretariat Library, Government of India, New Delhi, the year was 1955, and the post was Librarian Grade III. The interview went well until I faced the question, "In the absence of an inventory register, how will you conduct an inventory audit of the library?" I was despondent in my response, since I could not understand the question as I did not know the meaning of the term, 'inventory'. Sensing my predicament, the member putting that question reframed it by asking how you would take stock of the library in the absence of stock register. When I replied that every library will have its stock register, prompt came the reply from the member posing the question, assume that it is a hypothetical situation. After a long pause, I did answer the question clearly and correctly. The answer was that every book purchased by a library is accompanied by a bill (invoice), and from the bills one could recreate the stock register. The tense situation relaxed, and I could see smiles on the members' faces. My feeling was that the members, seeing my initial despondency, and the delay in answering had not expected that I would be able to answer the question to their satisfaction. The fact was that in those days library schools and librarians in India used the term stock register and stock-taking and not the term 'inventory', the commonly used term in the USA. It was natural for Mr. N.M. Ketkar, who had asked the question, to use the term 'inventory' with his MS degree in Library Science from the University of Columbia, and service at the US Information Centre, Bombay (now Mumbai) for many years.

Managerial insight : Language proficiency gives a person an added advantage over those less proficient in all walks of life, where communication is involved, and more so for those employed in service sectors. The library profession is no exception to this.

Language deficiency can scare away customers, lead to misunderstanding between parties in an engagement, and hamper progress in one's career. One can increase one's language skills and vocabulary strength by learning and exposure.

2. WHAT'S THERE IN SPELLING A PERSON'S NAME?

It was a practice in the Central Secretariat Library, Government of India to circulate a select number of magazines, particularly overseas journals on their receipt to a few officers of the rank of Secretary, Joint Secretary and Deputy Secretary located in the North and South Blocks of the Central Secretariat. Keeping to that practice, I sent a newly arrived journal issue to one of the Joint Secretary marking his name on the Circulation slip. It was a lengthy personal name in Urdu language, sounding like 'Ashfaque ——', with which I was unfamiliar. I had spelled his name erroneously on the circulation slip. A day later, Mr. Ketkar, the Chief Librarian, called me, and showed a note received from the official taking objection to spelling his name wrongly. He advised me to be careful in spelling the names, as a name not only identifies the individual, but also carries with it certain social and cultural values as well as sentiments. It had never occurred to me that people are very sensitive to their names, to their correct spelling and right pronunciation until this incident, and Mr. Ketkar's wise counsel.

Managerial insight : Proper use of language is a vital part of good communication. An individual's name is also associated with certain social and cultural values and sentiments. One needs to be conscious of the fact that names of persons carry with them a psychological note. Hence, one must adhere to proper pronunciation and correct spelling of a person's name, particularly so in an organizational context.

3. TECHNICAL TERMS VS. GENERAL VOCABULARY

A reader searching for books in the library on 'fire-control' systems, though they were in the library, could not locate any book on the subject on the shelves under the appropriate class number. This was due to wrong classification. It turned out that the books on *fire-control system* were filed along with the books on fire and firefighting. The mistake must have occurred due to the classifier not having the subject knowledge or classifying the book in a moment of absent mindedness. The two subjects are different and have different classification numbers. 'Fire-control system' is a technical term related to gun/weapons systems, whereas firefighting refers to measures taken to put out fires/ burning; the only common feature between the two terms being the word 'fire'. The mistake was rectified. How this incident became handy to find fault is given in Chap. 4.6.

Managerial insight : A classifier must have the basic knowledge of the subject domains with which the organization deals with; and be familiar with the technical terms of the field. In cases of doubt one can always seek the help of specialists in the field. The mistakes in classifying publications in libraries due to not understanding technical terms may happen sometimes. A misplaced book is a lost book. If such mistakes happen on a recurring basis, it will bring down the credibility of the library and affect its brand name.

4. VALUE OF LEARNING FOREIGN LANGUAGES.

Language being the most common medium of communication is central to all human interactions, and more so in today's world dominated by technology and globalization of economy. Though English continues to be the lingua franca of the world, other major languages like, Chinese, Japanese, Russian, German, French, Spanish, Arabic, and Hindi (and other major Indian languages) are gaining importance in conducting bilateral transactions and in accessing knowledge. My learning Russian and scientific German languages, at the elementary level, in the early part of my career, by attending courses conducted by The School of Foreign languages, Government of India, and the National Physical Laboratory Club, New Delhi, respectively had given me an additional advantage, where knowledge of Russian and German languages mattered. Apart from forming an item in the curriculum vitae, this language acquaintance helped me in making out what a given Russian or German title or text dealt with, while handling literature in these languages. In spite of the availability of automatic language translation facility now, it cannot fully match the advantages of natural language handling in live human interactions.

Managerial insight : Acquisition of additional language skills by members working in institutions and organizations, where they are required to interact with people belonging to different linguistic domains, is an enormous advantage to the organization. To encourage select employees to acquire required foreign language skills will benefit the organization. HRD departments of all progressive enterprises recognize this need.

5. MESMERIZING AN AUDIENCE

To come in contact with Shri B.S. Kesavan, (Padmashri), the Director of INSDOC, a leading personality that the library profession in India has seen, is a unique experience. Gifted in the use of English language, and a number of Indian languages including Kannada, Hindi, Tamil, Telugu and Bengali, one could feel that Saraswathi, the goddess of learning in Hindu Pantheon is speaking through him. On occasions, in speaking to his junior staff members he would use language terms which on the face of it would look like a tender rebuke, but the tone and the manner of delivery would be such that the other party would feel embedded affection in those words, and a feeling of nearness conveyed by them.

An unforgettable experience for those who attended the *Conference of Information Scientists*- March 1963 organized by the INSDOC/CSIR at Mysore was hearing Shri. Kesavan's address. One of his main objectives behind organizing that conference was to get it endorse his proposal to start a School of Information Science under INSDOC. However, a highly influential Head of another unit in the CSIR H.Q. was dead against the proposal. He gave a number of reasons why there was no need to start the school by INSDOC. His argument looked convincing to most participants. This was followed by Shri Kesavan at the mike. He began his speech praising the earlier speaker who had strongly opposed the proposal and the valuable points made by him. Many of us began to wonder then whether it was a volte-face on Shri. Kesavan's part. Then came his superb performance tearing into pieces the entire edifice built so cogently by the opposing party. The audience was thrilled. The proposal to start the course received overwhelming support. INSDOC started the Course and has filled the gap that existed in the area of advanced level training in information science. It is a sad thing that the course thus started has been abandoned recently.

Managerial insight : Good speech-making is an art. Not all leaders are endowed with that gift. By training and practice one can acquire that skill to some degree. A gifted orator can make even a most debatable issue convincing and worth supporting. Many novel ideas face still birth due to lack of effective communication and inability to spot the right sponsor.

6. ON LINGUISTIC INTOLERANCE

My professional career, as stated earlier, began at the Central Secretariat Library, Government of India in1955. Mr. Ketkar, the Chief Librarian had assigned me the work of managing periodicals section. One day Mr.Shivashankaran (name changed) an Assistant Librarian in another ministry of the Central Government came to me and started talking in Tamil language, non stop. I could not make out what he was talking about or what he wanted. I told him that I was not very familiar with Tamil language and requested him to speak in English. He took my not knowing Tamil as an offence committed by me and shouted at me: "it is a pity you don't know Tamil."..... "Who gave you the job?" I was really upset and asked him in return, did he know Kannada. He left the place with anger showing all over his face. I thought that was the end of it. The next day Mr. Ketkar called me and told that Mr. Shivashankaran had complained to him about the previous day's incident. I explained to him what had happened.

It is his greatness that he did not find fault with me. At the same time, he came out with words of wisdom and advice to me. The gist of his words of wisdom was that every language is to be respected; all languages are great by themselves; and language tolerance is an important virtue.

Managerial insight : Language is the main means of human communication. One's linguistic behaviour can make or mar good interpersonal relationship. Linguistic chauvinism and civil society don't go together. This is more so in our society, which is enriched from ancient times with many languages.

10

Career : Updating of Knowledge/Skills

Darwin's theory of 'survival of the fittest' applies equally to the survival of human societies and organizations made-up of individual members. The two main features of this game of survival and growth of organizations and individuals, seen particularly from the late twentieth century onwards, are the unprecedented increase in the rate of change taking place, and severe competition accompanying the change. The key to survival and progress in this environment lies in acquiring necessary knowledge and equipping oneself with the requisite training and experience, on a continuous basis all through one's career. According to M.B. Arthur career means the evolving sequence of a person's work experiences over time.[1] This follows from the profession chosen by the individual. An important feature of Western culture is the positive value attached to the concept of dignity of labour, which means that no work or profession is deemed low in status or undignified. The situation in our society is exactly opposite. If we are to progress, improve our economy and uphold equal rights of every citizen, it is imperative to accept and follow dignity of labour. Narrated here are a few incidents from my career, which also have a bearing on the Human Resource Development aspects of organizations.

1. WHY I JOINED THE LIBRARY PROFESSION

When I passed my 10th Standard examination, if I had tried, I could have become a doctor by joining the course of Licentiate in Medical Practice (LMP). Since I was averse to handling dead body organs and their dissection, I gave up the idea. As was the then prevailing attitude of middle class strata of society, the educational priority for the young was in the order of medicine, engineering, and science followed by commerce and arts. With the hope of becoming a scientist, I opted for physics, chemistry and mathematics as the subjects for my Intermediate level examination (now PUC/ 11th Standard) so that I could make my career in the field of chemistry, particularly by pursuing advanced research. Since I passed my Bachelor in Science (B.Sc.) degree in pass class, my joining Master in Science (M.Sc.) course in chemistry was out of question. With no other choice left, I joined as a teacher in the Viveka High School, Kota (in the present Dakshina Kannada district, Karnataka state) and served there for ten months. I could have continued in that line by studying for a Bachelor in Education (B.Ed.). Though I enjoyed teaching, I was looking for a line of career outside the beaten track. Since I was deeply interested in reading and acquiring knowledge, library had a special attraction for me from my childhood. It was then I saw the advertisement in a newspaper issued by the Benaras Hindu University, (BHU) inviting applications for admission to the Postgraduate Diploma in Library Science course. Without any second thoughts, I jumped at the opportunity by sending my application. I was selected and journeyed my way to Kashi/ Benaras (now Varanasi) in 1954. At that time I had no real idea about library science except the notion that I would be amidst books, and thus the opportunity to fulfill my desire to enter into the world of knowledge. It suited my temperament of treading a less beaten track, philosophic bent of mind (see also 2.4), individualistic and independent nature. Sixty years back any person going to Kashi and that too for study at BHU was considered both prestigious and holy. My going to Kashi became the talk of the town.

Several people had come to me with small amounts of money requesting me to offer it at the feet of Lord Vishwanath, on their behalf. A novice, not knowing the land and Hindi language, journeying to Kashi when the telephone and air service (the age of Dakota aircraft) were in their infancy, and with slim pocket was really an adventure; and I had always liked adventure. I owe it to my father that he allowed me to go to Kashi, though with a heavy heart and worried mind.

I consider that I was lucky to study in BHU. It is an experience difficult to describe— the most satisfying and enriching student life made possible by the caring professors, the eminent personalities associated with the University and their legacy, presence of students from different parts of the county, excellent hostel life, and the simple and understanding 'panditjis' running the messes and the tea shops.

The classes were held in the university library, and the teachers were Pandit D. Subramanyam, and Prof. C.G. Vishawanathan - the Librarian and the Assistant librarian, respectively. Both were great teachers and had the gift to make students understand the theories and functions of libraries, true sprit of librarianship, the responsibilities of librarians and the prospects in the field. More importantly, they (in particular Prof. Vishwanathan as he was also attending to the administrative side of the course) were always willing to hear the problems of students and help them. I also received a scholarship waiving the course fee. It is here that I met Mr. N.M. Ketkar, the Deputy Librarian, which resulted later in a mentor relationship (see 2.1, 9.6 and 12.1). To facilitate my getting a job after obtaining the Diploma, I needed some practical experience to include in my curriculum vitae. When I broached this topic with Prof. C.G., he allowed me to work on a voluntary basis in different sections of the library for three months. My career entry into the profession of library and information science began in 1955 with my joining the Central Secretariat Library, Government of India, and New Delhi in 1955 as Librarian Grade-III.

Managerial insight : In choosing a career, one is guided by several factors. These include- one's desire and ambition, parental influences, academic strength, financial position, perception of present and future prospects in the field. After choosing a career, it does not take much time to find out whether it is satisfying, and if not, try another after careful assessment of the situation. However, one should remember the saying "a rolling stone does not gather mass".

2. A PERSONALITY ASSESSMENT GAME

In April 1981, I attended a two week Management and Work-study Appreciation Course at the Defence Institute of Work-study, Mussoorie. We were about twenty officers coming from different establishments of the DRDO. At the end of the course, a management game was conducted for the participants. It is based on the theory that living together for two weeks in the Institute's Hostel in close proximity and attending the classes together provided the opportunity to each participant to interact with other participants. Thus, it was expected that because of personal interaction and observations each officer would be in a position to assess the personality, character and attainments of every other participant. The game consisted of asking every candidate to express in five minutes his candid assessment of the personality and behavioural traits of every other person in the group, by turns. One of the strict rules of the game was that each speaker must speak up only the positive aspects of the person commented upon, and refrain from expressing any negative opinions. The first person called to make the assessment was the senior most participant in the class, who in turn, after his presentation, would name the next speaker.

Though it is a game, if properly conducted, it can serve as a useful personality assessment technique based on multiple feedbacks resulting from community living for a few days. It also acts as a useful break introducing a little fun in an otherwise hard programme. For the individual participant the reading reflects his personality horoscope as cast by co-participants.

Managerial insight : Often, one will not know one's strengths and weaknesses unless some one else points them out. Such assessments will help one to make a self introspection, and provide an opportunity to self-correction/improvement. But such evaluations to be useful must come from persons of integrity having no positive or negative bias towards the person commented upon. The true picture of one's personality as seen by others would emerge only if the whole exercise is conducted in secret, and the criterion is not restricted to the expression of only positive aspects of the person. One must consider such assessments with an open mind and not get prejudiced, even if it is adverse in nature.

3. AN ERRATIC CAREER EXPERIENCE

I was selected for the post of Senior Technical Assistant in the Information Department of the Tata Iron and Steel Company (TISCO) at Jamshedpur, one of the prestigious industrial concerns of India. At that period of time, someone getting a job in a Tata enterprise was considered lucky. With tremendous enthusiasm and expectations I went to join the post. At first, I was taken to the Senior Administrative Officer of the Company. The meeting was really interesting as well as satisfying for me. It created a feeling of delight in joining such an enlightened and progressive enterprise. He briefed me on the history and the working of the factory, vision and values driving the company, and the future prospects in the Department. It was an excellent briefing for any new entrant. Then I was taken to the Information Department for reporting to duty. After a brief meeting with the Information Officer (IO), a journalist by profession in his early seventies, I was asked to meet Mr.Ramesh Bhandari (name changed), the Assistant Information Officer (AIO) under whom I was to work.

Mr. Bhandari spent almost two hours with me on 'briefing'. It all centered around two points: a) how the IO was pampered by the management by giving a fat salary and perks for doing nothing other than bringing out a weekly Technical Information bulletin, and b) he who is doing the real work and manages the library is treated badly both by the IO and higher management. More shocking aspect of the 'briefing' was that he said nothing much about the functioning of the library, its objectives and services, and my responsibilities in the library. I was assigned some routine work, which did not require much of my time or aptitude. The daily lunch hour was spent mostly in small talk, often mixed with juicy tales. The other colleague was a young, enthusiastic and also professionally trained person, who adored Dr. S.R.Ranganathan, but had lost his way in the stale environment of the department. It was not surprising that I made the decision on the very first day of joining the Department that it was not the organization for me to work, and I must quit the job the very first opportunity I get. Meanwhile, the Head of Planning Department invited me to join him, which I rejected. The main reason for me to quit TISCO was the industrial environment that prevailed at that time.

However, my stay there was fruitful to me in many ways. I specially concentrated on preparing annotative bibliographies and reading lists on different aspects of steel making technology, industrial engineering and management, which were of direct interest to technical and managerial personnel of the company. My stay there gave me the first hand experience of working in a factory environment, and a chance to observe or think about how a vast industrial enterprise is run. I could also get a little peep into the psychology of workers and midlevel managerial cadre. A common fact I noticed was that in spite of Tata's enlightened management policies, and their caring for workers' wellbeing there seemed to be a deep sense of dissatisfaction among workers. I was exposed to the discipline of management science, and see how it is applied and works in the real world. This industrial background and the knowledge of management science I learnt there was of immense help to me in framing the course content for my lectures on modern management to the students of newly started M.Lib.Sc. course at the University of Poona, many years later.

Managerial insight : The first day in a job in one's career is often turns out to be of special significance. Job satisfaction is a dominant factor in continuing with one's job. A frustrated leadership is a de-motivating factor in any organization. Even a worst situation has its own plus points, if only we care to think.

4. A WRONG CHOICE OF CAREER. IMPLICATIONS FOR ORGANIZATIONS

An interview was held for filling the post of Senior Scientific Assistant (SSA) in the library of IAT. Except Mr.Vinod Kumar (name changed), all other candidates who appeared for the interview had library qualifications with a degree in science. Mr. Kumar, who belonged to 'backward community' did not have library qualification, but had a good Master's degree in chemistry. The Committee was to decide between a candidate with library degree and the one with M.Sc. Most of the members on the Committee were in favour of selecting a library trained person. However, I convinced the Committee to select Mr.Kumar. I had in my mind that Mr. Kumar, under proper guidance could be shaped into a first class information scientist, who would be in a position to create new information products of value to the users of the library.

Before joining the library he came to me to seek some assurances. Since his appointment letter stated that the post is purely temporary he was worried that his services may be terminated at any time after his joining. I explained to him that a large number of posts and new appointments in the central government are of temporary tenure, but surly they would be made permanent in course of time. No employee's services are terminated unless he or she commits serious offences like theft or fraud. In the hindsight it appears to me that my assurances were uncalled for.

From day one of his joining the library, he showed no interest in work. He was always talking about making a career in the field of chemistry. He used to spend considerable time in the Faculty of Chemistry lobbying for his transfer to that faculty. Any amount of advice and persuasion from me and my senior colleague had any effect on him. Even my sincere suggestion that I would support him, if he wanted to become an abstractor for the prestigious *Chemical Abstracts* published by the American Chemical Society so that he can improve his career prospects had no impact on him. A stage was reached when he became a serious liability to the library. Any amount of advice, coaxing, pleading and threat of termination of service did not make him mend his attitude. The breaking point was reached when he dumped into dust bin a huge number of catalogue cards instead of filing them- a serious lapse in work.

Following this incidence, he was served with a notice of "under observation" for three months to improve himself. However, there was not even a little change in his attitude towards work. I was left with no other choice but to ask for terminating his service. Then I told the Chairman, Library Committee, my immediate reporting officer about terminating the services of Mr. Kumar. He was worried about of Mr. Kumar making it a case of victimization due to cast prejudice and its consequences. After discussing the issue thread bear with the Chief Administrative Officer, I initiated action to terminate the services of Mr. Kumar.

A Committee was constituted by the Director to review the case. Following the review, Mr. Kumar was issued the order terminating his service. Immediately, he came to me pleading for the withdrawal of the order, as otherwise he and his family would be on the streets. I was in a grave dilemma as the situation juxtaposed two contradictory value positions before me: a) upholding discipline and the interest of the institution, and b) human consideration. I had to find a means that served both the interests.

Termination of service would leave a black mark in Kumar's career record. A part solution to the problem was to offer him the choice of voluntary resignation, to which he readily agreed. But the problem was accepting his voluntary resignation in place of termination of service required the approval of the Director. I explained the position to Mr. B.R.Sagar, the Chief Administrative Officer and requested him to talk to the Director on the issue. Air Cdre. S.K. Nair, the Director at the that time, and a person of rare leadership qualities, agreed to the proposal of accepting Mr. Kumar's voluntary resignation- all this happened within two hours. Regarding his finding a new job, Mr. Desai, my colleague, had known that Mr. Kumar was selected to the post of SSA by another defence establishment in Pune, but they had withheld issuing the appointment letter to him for some reason. I requested Mr. Desai, a resourceful person and of helping nature, to use his efforts to expedite the process of issuing the appointment letter from the other establishment. Mr. Desai succeeded in his efforts and Mr. Kumar joined the new establishment within a week. It is to the credit of Mr. Kumar that he did not raise, even indirectly, the issue of discrimination and prejudice at any point of time.

Managerial insight : Use of non-cooperation in work as a strategy rarely works. Of course, it depends on the strength of character of the persons involved in such conflicts and the culture of the organization. In employer-employee conflicts, human aspect needs to be taken into consideration while terminating services. This may not be so in Western work culture, but Indian social conditions imply otherwise, within certain limits. In choosing a career one needs to be careful. Given the employment conditions in India many are forced to take up any offer of job that comes there way irrespective of whether it suits them or not. This leads to all sorts of problems to the employee as well as employer, which can be avoided by making the right choice, even though it may involve some waiting period.

Even in bureaucracy, barring a few exceptions, all members are open minded and are always guided by higher human values and governance ethics. Every problem has a right or workable solution. Only we have to think and approach the problem with a positive frame of mind. Loyalty to the organization which is often sidelined is an important attribute of a good worker. Self belief is another factor that gives the manager the moral strength to pursue right action based on sound decisions overcoming hindrances created by all sorts of vested interests. It also means that the initiator of such action must be prepared to sacrifice self-interest. It is only persons of high integrity overcoming these weaknesses keeps the organization moving in the right path.

5. LOYALTIES TO THE ORGANIZATION

Miss. Radhika Chowdri (name changed) joined the IAT library as a Junior Technical Assistant. She was intelligent, had initiative and capable of achieving goals. I thought she could be shaped to make her an asset to the library. After two years of service she was deputed to undergo one year advanced training program in documentation conducted by INSDOC, New Delhi. It needed special efforts to get the government approval to sponsor her for the course. After her return form the course she was provided with ample work opportunities to apply her talent and new ideas learnt from attending the course and contribute to the innovative growth of the library and information service. She was also promoted to the next higher grade. However, she applied for a higher post in a CSIR laboratory, got selected, and wanted to leave IAT. There was an impediment to relieve her from the service of DRDO as she had executed a bond to serve DRDO for 3 years as a precondition to her being sponsored to the INSDOC course. I was not happy with her leaving as IAT had taken care of all her genuine career interests. When the administration insisted on completing 3 year bond period I was able to persuade the administrative authorities of the Institute (Shri. B.R.Sagar, the CEO) to waive off the bond period in view of CSIR being an autonomous body under the Government of India. A year after joining the new establishment she found her new place of work intolerable. She wrote to me telling her woes and requesting me to help her return to IAT. She could rejoin as she had a lien on her post in IAT, but there was a hitch in re-accommodating her in the library, which was also overcome. However, she left the job after working for a total period of about three and a half years thus nullifying all the efforts and resources incurred on her to make her serve the institution better.

Managerial insight : Loyalty is a reciprocal phenomenon between the workers and the enterprises including the state and its organs, corporate bodies and the like which is collectively represented by its executives/bureaucrats, board of directors etc. Any mismatch between one's ability and ambition is bound to affect his or her career plans adversely, even in the best of circumstances. The best of intentions sometimes go astray in ensuring right returns.

6. FEAR OF FAILURE

I was preparing for the job interview scheduled for the next day. The interview was for a mid-level position in an international organization. The Director of INSDOC, New Delhi where I was working at that time had recommended five names that included my name and four of my senior colleagues in the organization for consideration. A day before the interview we were informed that there is a written test prior to the interview.

At the appointed time all the five of us appeared for the written test. It was not like a school examination which is conducted under invigilation. We were busy writing the test paper. When we were in the middle of the test, the Staff Officer to the Director accompanied by another person entered the room unnoticed by us. Apparently they had walked in to see how the test was proceeding. They saw Mr. Gopal Krishnan (name changed), engaged in copying answers from the person sitting next to him. This was reported to the Director. Apparently the person who accompanied the Staff Officer was from the international organization. No one was selected for the post.

The following morning the Director called us to express his anguish over the incident. He felt sorry that he was let down by us before a foreign dignitary by the shameful act of one of us. It was at his suggestion that the international organization had shown interest in offering a position to a candidate from INSDOC.

Success and failure are common occurrences in life. Success generally brings euphoria and may lead to striving for further success. Failure, on the other hand, may lead to agony, loss of self confidence and finally fear. What about fear of failure? Fear seems to be more harmful than failure. Fear can lead to several unpredictable consequences of which one is cited above.

Managerial insight : Gopal Krishnan's copying act is inexplicable. Since I knew him well for long I could vouch that his fraudulent act was definitely not in tune with his character. It is difficult to believe that he was motivated by the lure of the post. It could not be accounted as a chance occurrence as he was a responsible person with over 25 years of service put in different organizations. Most probably it was an impetuous act powerfully driven by acute fear, the fear of falling in the esteem of the Director. He knew that the Director had very high opinion about his abilities and character, and thus expectations. One explanation could be that he was afraid that a bad performance in the written test would terribly affect his standing in the eyes of the Director. This is a case of severe mismatch between one's self perceived ability and his or her self perceived expectations of his higher-ups leading to fear, and the fear driving to an act of misconduct.

7. PROFESSIONAL PRIDE

The Military Engineering Service (MES) at one time had the unsavory reputation of being corrupt. Whether it was true or not, that image got stuck in the minds of general public. This bug had caught me too, while I was serving in the Institute of Armament Technology, Poona.

As Head of Library and Information Centre, I had to deal occasionally with the local unit of the MES for maintenance of the building, repair and replacement of nonworking utilities. On one occasion, the Assistant Garrison Engineer had come to see some installations in the Library. I had accompanied him to show the place. While on inspection, I showed him a portion of a wall where rain water had seeped in and was affecting the storage of books. I should have been wise enough to leave it at that and concentrate on getting it repaired. Instead, I made some loose remarks about the MES service and the corruption. His reaction was instantaneous. Seething with anger, he exploded at me for making allegations of corruption without proof, and passing judgment on the quality of work without having the requisite knowledge and expertise. I apologized to him for my loose remarks, irrespective of truth or lack of it in my remarks. It was a lesson for me, learnt the hard way.

Managerial insight : No one tolerates others making unsavory comments on one's profession. Similarly, no one likes casting aspersions on one's professional ability and competency. Before leveling a charge against another person/agency one must be sure of the facts leading to the charge.

8. KNOWLEDGE/SKILLS UPDATING AND CONTINUOUS TRAINING

Continued education and training of employees is a key factor in the growth process of an organization and also the employees. However, one must be clear about the purpose for which he or she wants to update her or his knowledge base. Equally important is how the newly acquired knowledge and skill is put into practice. Acquisition of knowledge and skill by an organization's employees through further education and training at the organization's expense is of limited use to the organization, unless it leads to improvement, creation of new knowledge, its dissemination and sharing, and development of new skills to the advantage of the organization and society. Cited here are a few cases.

When one attends a training course, it is essential to be clear about the purpose of her or his participation in the course. Then, one will be able to concentrate on those aspects of the course which will help in achieving the set objectives. If there is no precise set objective in mind then one has to look for work areas where what is learnt during the course can be usefully applied. Applying the knowledge and skills learnt by attending such programs, after careful assessment of pros and cons, is sure to benefit the organization.

(a) Why I Did a COBOL Programming Course : I was one among the three officers from IAT selected to undergo a 5 week COBOL Programming Course in 1974 conducted by the Computer Centre, Armament Research and Development Establishment, (ARDE) Poona. It was the era of the first generation computers, when a computer occupied a whole room. At that time there were only a few computers in the whole country. The software programs in use were COBOL for general purpose applications and FORTRAN for scientific purposes.

In the last phase of the course the participants were divided into small groups of 4 or 5 persons, and each group was assigned the task of building a small program. I did try to learn the computational techniques that went into the program, but lacked the requisite temperament. I was keen on knowing the general principles underlying the operation of a computer, what a computer can and cannot do, where it can be usefully employed, in what manner data is to be provided to the programmer, the output form and the like. I did get a good grasp of what I wanted to know. My whole purpose was to know whether a computer can be used in a library, and if so how I must approach the actual programmer. At the end of the course there was the feedback session. Each participant was required to give his or her impressions on the course. When my turn came I began by telling the fact that I did not learn much about the actual building of a program. The Head of CC was aghast by my statement and before his proceeding further, I stated the fact that I was not to become a programmer and my interest was in knowing the capabilities of a computer and its applications. I explained how important the course had been to me viewed from a manager's perspective of applying COBOL program in IAT library. I could sense a feeling of relief and satisfaction on his face. It is this course and the software program developed by the ARDE Computer Centre that enabled us later to successfully apply computer in IAT Information Centre and Library.

With my experience of attending professional training programs and its benefit to the organization and self, I firmly believed that it is a part of my duty to encourage members working with me to update their knowledge by further education, improve their skills by attending professional training courses, and to get exposed to the best practices by visiting other institutions known for their high standards of performance, through official sponsorship. I was successful in converting my belief into action to a large extent.

Managerial insight : Healthy development of an organization and its people is interdependent, but the organization is above the individual. As an enterprise grows, its employees benefit in terms of increased opportunities, material gains and greater esteem. Development of individuals working in an organization, in turn, adds to the further growth of the organization in terms of bringing more innovations, increased productivity, new knowledge generation and enhancement of its brand value. Education never goes waste, and learning has no age bar. However, one must be clear about the purpose for which he or she wants to update his or her knowledge-base and undergo training programs. Acquisition of knowledge and skill by an employee through further education and training is of limited use, unless it leads to further creation of knowledge, its dissemination and sharing, and development of new skills to the advantage of the organization and society. The manager has a responsibility in providing the requisite means of fulfilling this objective.

(b) Enrolment for Doctoral Programme : From the early days of my entering library profession, the claim often made that librarianship is a knowledge-based profession, and libraries are disseminators of knowledge had bothered me. At least until the middle of my career, my experience of working in different libraries and documentation centres led me to infer that library profession is all about managing a setup dealing with books, journals and other forms of printed publications and not actual knowledge, except to a limited extent 'reference service'. Even a cursory glance at epistemology, the branch of philosophy that deals with the study of knowledge strengthened my reservations. It was this longstanding doubt about the claim that created in me a strong desire to delve deep into the subject of knowledge, its characteristics and its relationship with other branches of knowledge, particularly library and information science. This was the genesis of my taking up research on this topic at the doctorate level. But to pursue a doctoral program a master's degree is a prerequisite. Given my other commitments, I was not in a position to take up M.Lib.Sc. course as a fulltime pursuit. It is at this juncture, I learnt about the M.Lib.Sc. program of the University of Bombay with emphasis on self-study, minimizing the lecture-sessions, which suited my requirements. After completing the M.Lib.Sc. Course from the University of Bombay, I registered for Ph.D. program of the University of Poona.

Two crucial elements a student faces in pursuing a doctoral program are: selection of the guide, and the selection of a suitable topic for research. I was very particular that the guide I choose must be a real scholar and a real teacher. When I went to register for the doctoral program at the University of Poona, one of the teachers there tried to persuade me to select him as my guide, but I was very keen on Prof. B. Anderson of Bombay University, recognized as a guide by the Poona University, to be my guide. Fortunately for me, Prof. Anderson made an exception in agreeing to be my guide. Sadly, Prof. Anderson had been ailing and bedridden a few days before my submitting the thesis. It fell on Prof. M.R. Riswadkar, the reader and a great teacher in the Dept. of Library and Information Science of the University to see through my submitting the thesis.

On the selection of topics for the study I tentatively thought of two topics- a) Indo-US librarianship, and b) Knowledge and its characteristics. Prof. Anderson had no objection to my choosing either of the two. The latter theme was chosen for the reasons that the first topic did not seem to be very challenging, whereas knowledge as the topic of study had always interested me and would be relatively more challenging. But there seemed to be a hitch in the Department of Library and Information Science in accepting the topic 'Knowledge and its Characteristics', as the subject comes under the jurisdiction of the Faculty of Philosophy. To overcome this hurdle the topic was changed to 'Information as a Commodity: An Inquiry into the Characteristics of Knowledge'. Prof. Riswadkar, who had always shown keen interest in my academic pursuits readily agreed to the change and got it accepted by the authorities. The changed title was quite befitting as the study of the characteristics of information and information services, and the economic characteristics of knowledge and information together formed the major portion of the thesis. Later, 'Indo-U.S. Librarianship' was taken up as the topic for the doctoral program by one of my students at the M.Lib.I.Sc.

My taking up Ph.D. program was solely for my inner satisfaction, and fulfillment of a long standing desire. There was no compelling reason for me to do it. In fact, I received the degree just a year before my retirement from service. However, my registering for Ph.D. immensely helped me to visit USA as a Fulbright scholar. As stated earlier, my topic for Ph.D. was the study of information as a commodity. What better place is there in the world to study commodity aspect of information than USA? This factor must also have influenced my selection for the Fulbright fellowship.

Visit to USA. It was a unique experience for me. As far as fulfilling my research interest was concerned, I was able to observe/study the working of major libraries- public and institutional, and the quality of service rendered by them. With some help from my friend R.N. Paul, involved in information industry and settled in America, I was able to meet and discuss with persons associated with some of the leading enterprises that were producing and marketing information in different forms, on the commodity aspects of information and knowledge, and the larger issue of information component in the US economy. My observations, studies and experiences in U.S also helped enrich my lectures on management, and in incorporating the results of my in-depth study into my doctoral work.

Apart from the academics part of my visit, what impressed

me most were the work culture of USA laid on the foundation of trust, duty consciousness and helpfulness sans display of emotions governing public-citizen and customer-trade contacts, environment consciousness, and placing community interest above individual's interest seen in all aspects of American life. A Fulbright scholar is also a cultural ambassador of his country. The talk I gave on *Daivada puje* (a form of worship of local deities prevalent in south coastal Karnataka) evinced keen interest among the American audience present there. When I pointed out that even Christian community living in this part of India are greatly influenced by these beliefs, many among the audience would not believe it. They were astonished when I cited from the matrimonial columns appearing in many leading news papers in India carrying advertisements "wanted a Catholic Brahmin bride for a Catholic Brahmin boy..." It was Dr. Om Sharma and his wife Mrs.Vimla Sharma from the University of Michigan Library, who treated me as a part of their family, and provided me the opportunity to see a bit of American social norms and value system.

(c) The Challenge of Continuing Education : The importance of upgrading of knowledge and skills by the employees of an organization as an ongoing process- the spirit of which I imbibed from Dr. Nanda (see11.2) - is realized when the employees take up the pursuit seriously. Narrated here is one such instance. Mrs. Shanthamani has been working as a clerk in the library of ADE for many years. She had all the qualities to empower herself by upgrading her educational qualifications and improve her career prospects. When I impressed upon her the need for updating her knowledge base, particularly in library science, she had serious reservations about my stand. Given her full time engagement in the library and the responsibility of running the house hold, it was not easy for her to think of taking up an additional venture. She had to decide whether she wants to remain as a junior clerk and retire, at the most, as a head clerk or become a professional and retire as an officer, and have the satisfaction of serving readers in a better capacity. I impressed upon her to think over it and take a call. On my part I assured her all possible help from my side. It is to her credit that she took up the challenge, worked doggedly and obtained her degree in library science through distance education/open University. With her library science degree she became a technical assistant, involving a change of cadre from clerical to technical, very soon.

Some twenty years after my retirement from ADE, one day, I was surprised to receive a telephone call from Mrs. Shanthamani, informing me that she wants to meet me. She came in the evening accompanied by two of her colleagues. She wanted to tell me in person about her promotion as a technical officer and express her gratitude to me. She said that she is able to contribute substantially to the services rendered to the users of KC, because of her educational pursuit while in service. She was generous to attribute her becoming an officer and the opportunity she got to contribute to the functioning of KC solely to my early guidance and persuasion to take-up further studies. Moreover, she said that following the path set by her, two other persons in the establishment have got empowered through continuing education.

Managerial insight : Education never goes waste. There is no age bar to acquire new knowledge and skills. What is needed to update one's knowledge thorough continuing education is intense desire and perseverance. Updating of one's knowledge benefits not only the individual, but also the organization where she or he is serving. Acquisition of new knowledge/skills, if it is to serve the interests of the organization, has to be need-oriented and properly directed.

9. MEMBERSHIP OF ISI SUB-COMMITTEE ON DOCUMENTATION

While working in IAT, on the recommendation of Shri. B.S.Kesavan, Director of INSDOC, the Indian Standards Institution (ISI), New Delhi, appointed me as a member of the Documentation Sectional Committee EC-2. The ISI requested me to attend the meeting scheduled to be held in Delhi. I sent a note through proper channel seeking permission to take part in the activities of the sub-committee, and also approval of my move to Delhi on temporary duty to attend the meeting. The Deputy Dean and Chairman, Library Committee, my immediate higher authority, returned the note stating that my participation in the Committee is not of any benefit to the Institute, and only benefits me in my personal capacity. I was taken aback at his segregating institutional benefit from that of individual's personal benefit. I sent back the note explaining that membership in a national body like ISI is a recognition of IAT as an institution of eminence, and a recognition of my ability to contribute to their work, which is of national importance; and also the fact that I had no personal role in ISI selecting me as a member of the Sub-Committee. More importantly, no institution can derive benefit unless the individual member of the organization first acquires the pertinent knowledge and then applies it to the working of the organization. That is how the phenomena of knowledge acquisition and transfer work. My acceptance of membership in the Sub-Committee, as well as my temporary duty move to Delhi was approved by the Dean overruling the Deputy Dean's negative remarks on my note.

Managerial insight : The progress of an organization, to a large extent, depends on the caliber of its employees and their knowledge and skill/expertise-base. Enlightened organizations plan and support its employees to acquire knowledge and skills relevant to the efficient and creative functioning of the organization as an ongoing process. Unless the individual first acquires knowledge and skill beneficial to the organization, it cannot be applied or transferred to the organization. The yardstick to be applied in such cases is to ascertain how far such acquisition of knowledge and skill is relevant to the organization, and in what manner it adds value to its functioning and its image. If it is of benefit only to the individual, the organization may not come in the way of the individual acquiring additional knowledge, but not allow it at the monetary expense of the organization. This is the principle behind the managements of forward-looking organizations granting sabbatical leave to its functionaries.

9.1. Calling it a Day

My active career which began in 1954 came to a close in 1991— spanning a period of nearly 37 years, which began as Librarian Grade-III in the Central Secretariat library, New Delhi and ending up as Scientist E, Head of Knowledge Centre,

Aeronautical Development Establishment (ADE), Bangalore. The end was abrupt and of my choice. If I wanted to I could have continued in ADE for another ten months. I opted for voluntary retirement. The reason for this was that I found the work environment in the establishment under the then Director, as far as I was concerned, was not conducive for creative and dedicated work (see 4.6 and 12.7) By continuing there, I was sure, that I would not be able to contribute much to the organization other than passing time and drawing salary, and thereby compromising with my integrity- personal as well as professional, and doing injustice to self and the organization. My only regret at the time of leaving the Establishment was that I could not introduce the barcode system for identifying books for use in issue and return counter management, which would have also helped in annual stock taking of library holdings (see 3.6 b).

Managerial insight : One who is born has to die one day or the other. So also one's career has to have an end. The question is to decide when to call it off. The right time is when one looks back and reviews his or her career years spent so far and gets the sure feeling that further continuing in the enterprise results only in diminishing returns to the enterprise and lack of feeling of satisfaction to self. An important factor that goes to influence the quit decision will be the financial status of the individual. It is better for the concerned individual to call it the end of day before the enterprise serves the quit notice or makes the working environment a hell. However, this should not mean the end of active life or the end of pursuing other interests one likes. A happy career is one where the concerned individual gets the feeling that it was quite rewarding both for the concerned individual and the employing enterprise/organization.

REFERENCES

1. Arthur, M.B. Intelligent enterprises, intelligent careers. Academy of Management Executive 9(4): 7-20, 1995.

11

Recognizing and Rewarding Merit

One of the characteristics that distinguish great leaders from the ordinary is their acumen to recognize merit and express it through action. This rare leadership quality discerned from the acts of four great personalities- Shri B.S. Kesavan (Padma Shri), Dr. J.N. Nanda, Air.Cdr.S.K.Nair (AVSM) and Maj. Gen. Subba Rao (AVSM) are narrated here.

1. VISIT OF HON. MINISTER M.C. CHAGLA TO THE DOCUMENTATION UNIT

This incident happened in 1965 when I was serving as Documentation Officer/ Scientist B in the Publications and Information Division (PID), New Delhi- a unit of the Council of Scientific and Industrial Research (CSIR), New Delhi. I had then put in just about two and a half years of service there. I was selected by the Union Public Service Commission (UPSC), with the additional grant of two increments, for the post of Scientist 'C' in the Institute of Armament Studies at Pune- a higher Institute of education under the Defence Research and Development Organization (DRDO), Government of India. During those days a selection by the UPSC was considered a hallmark of high recognition. At that time Shri. B.S. Kesavan (Padma Shri) was the Director of the Indian National Scientific

Documentation Centre (INSDOC), present National Institute of Science Communication and Information (NISCAIR), another unit of CSIR. He also held temporary charge of PID. Shri Kesavan wanted to retain my services at PID. At that point of time, Hon. M.C. Chagla, the then Vice-President of CSIR and also the Minister for Law in the Central cabinet was visiting INSDOC. After his visit to INSDOC, Shri Kesavan brought Hon. Chagla to my Unit. He was explained the work and the services provided by the Documentation Unit. Mr. Kesavan briefed him on the excellent work done by the unit. He also placed before him the latest article[1] of mine published in the prestigious *International Review of Documentation* (*Revu de la Documatacio*). Just when Hon. Chagla was leaving the Unit, Mr. Kesavan, in a matter of fact manner, told him that he was unable to retain me in CSIR anymore. Hon. Chagla asked the reason for it. Shri. Kesavan explained the situation. Hon. Chagla's decision was spontaneous. He asked the Director to put up the case for my retention in PID by creating a post of Scientist C. Within a week the order promoting me as Scientist C reached me. This happened at a time (Indo-Pakistan War period) when there was a ban on creating new posts or filling existing vacancies in the Government of India and its affiliated bodies, like CSIR. However, due to strong personal reasons I did not stay in CSIR. It was also at this juncture that Dr. S.R.Ranganathan invited me to join DRTC at Bangalore as a faculty member, which too I could not accept.

2. DR. J. N. NANDA'S LETTER TO H.Q.

In the 1970s, avenues for promotion in the scientific cadre in the DRDO were extremely dim; and one had to wait for 12 to 15 years for the next promotion. At that time I had put in a service of just 6 years in IAT/DRDO. Dr. J.N. Nanda, a distinguished scientist with a number of awards for indigenous development of export substitute materials for use in the three services to his credit, became the Director and Dean of IAT. He was a firm believer in the need for continuous education of the staff. Time and again he used to impress upon the scientific staff members, particularly the young and those in the junior ranks, that they must update their knowledge in their respective fields through further studies so essential to remain competent in a fast changing technological world. This had considerable impact on the young members of the faculties. I imbibed this ethos from him, and made it a principle to help my junior co-workers to update their knowledge and skills through continuous education and training. Being a regular user of the library, he had made a good assessment of the library, its services and its management.

One day, at the closing hours of the library, I received a cover marked 'confidential' from the Director's Secretariat. In it was the copy of Dr. Nanda's letter addressed to the DRDO headquarters (H.Q.) recommending immediate promotion to me in recognition of the outstanding contributions made by the library to the teaching and research efforts of the Institute. The letter also included another scientist's name recommended for promotion on the grounds that he was retiring in 18 months after serving the DRDO conscientiously without getting a well deserved promotion even after a wait of 15 years. The incident left a deep impression on me for the sole reason that it was an exceptional gesture on the part of the Director entirely based on his own assessment, and devoid of any external influence. It is a different matter that the letter made no impact at the H.Q.

3. AIR.CDR. S.K.NAIR, (AVSM) WRITING TO H.Q.

This is an incident that happened in1978. The DRDO H.Q. released the list of scientists who were promoted to the next higher grades. The list included a few names from IAT including mine. I was promoted and posted to DESIDOC, Delhi. Immediately on receipt of the order, Air Cdr. Nair, the then Director and Dean wrote to the H.Q. strongly recommending that Narayana must be posted back to IAT in the interest of the institution. I had no idea that such a recommendation had gone from IAT. I came to know of this only later, when I received a copy of the letter sent to H.Q. signed by Air Cmdr Nair. The H.Q. cancelled my posting to DESIDOC, and I continued to serve at IAT.

Managerial insight : It is difficult to find an appropriate term that explains the managerial psychology behind such acts. Surely it is not generosity, and, may be, it is a part of managerial ethics of the highest order. For me, its greatness lies more in the value behind the spontaneous gestures shown by the leadership, and not necessarily in the result of the act.

4. MAJ. GEN. N.SUBBA RAO'S (AVSM) RECOMMENDATION

The DRDO instituted in 1983 two categories of annual awards to recognize and honour those DRDO scientists and engineers who had made outstanding contributions towards defence efforts. The award was to be given to one person in each major area of activity. The award consisted of two categories: *Scientist of the Year* award, and cash award, the former being the more prestigious one. Of the select areas, one was 'Information and Training'. There were a few candidates in the reckoning from IAT for the awards. Maj.Gen.N. Subba Rao (AVSM), the then Director and Dean, it seems, recommended two names from IAT for the *Scientist of the Year* awards. One was my name in recognition of my contributions in the field of 'Information and Training', and the other name, I was told, was from metallurgy. I was selected for the S*cientist of the year*- 1983 award. The awards were presented by the then Hon. Prime Minister of India, Smt. Indira Gandhi in New Delhi on 13th January, 1984.

5. REWARDING EXCELLENCE: CASE OF MR. SIDDHU

Mr. A.S. Siddhu had been working as a Cataloguer in the Documentation Unit (DU) of Publications and Information Directorate (PID), Council of Scientific and Industrial Research, New Delhi for more than 15 years. The posts of Cataloguer and Upper Division Clerk (UDC) were of the same rank and were inter-transferable. The designation of the post went with the place of work, i.e. Documentation Unit or Administration. PID was set up to publish *The Wealth of India*—A multi-volume encyclopaedia of Indian raw materials and industrial products, besides publishing scientific journals. The DU was created to collect, organize and provide requisite information needed by the editorial staff.

Though Mr. Siddhu was only a matriculate (present day 10th Standard), his knowledge of plant taxonomy and information on Indian plant raw materials was truly astounding. This was vouched for by the fact that many times editors consulted him to get their doubts on taxonomical position of plants clarified. He was an outstanding worker. Though his talent, knowledge and contributions were recognized, appreciated and he was promised promotion by previous heads of DU, the reward remained only a promise. Evidently, they were constrained by the facts that he did not fulfill the required minimum qualification of a degree in science, and also getting him promoted involved change of cadre from clerical to scientific, which needed special sanction. I wanted to rectify this situation. When I told him that justice would be done to him, he only laughed it away saying that every previous Head had said the same thing.

By a happy coincidence PID was put under the Director, Indian National Scientific Documentation Centre (INSDOC), headed by Mr. B.S.Kesavan (Padma Shri), a distinguished librarian, enlightened leader and dynamic manager. When I raised Siddhu's case with him, he was convinced of the merit of the case and asked me to put up the case file. The remarkable aspect of the decision, as felt by me, was that the Director asked me only one question and that was whether I was fully justified in recommending promotion to Siddhu. Within a week, Mr. Siddhu, the cataloguer became a Junior Scientific Assistant – a rare case of talent recognition and converting the recognition into reward. The incident happened some fifty years ago. He later retired as Scientist B.

Managerial insight : One may identify talent in an organization but converting that recognition to reward needs extraordinary quality of mind on the part of the top executive. This is particularly so in relatively rigid organizational setups and in societies where caste and language factors play their influences, apart from vested interests subverting fair treatment. Effective organizations are built on trust and integrity of their people, and not by those who become disgruntled due to lack of appreciation of their outstanding contributions and deprivation of just reward.

6. LIBRARY WINS A PRIZE: IKEBANA COMPETITION

Ladies Club of IAT/ Welfare Association of IAT held an Ikebana (Japanese flower arrangement) competition. It was held at the library premises. I felt that the library must participate in it. With the resources available within the premises, the library put up an exhibit. There were nearly 50 participants. The exhibit from the library received the third prize.

Managerial insight : Library being a part of the community, it is desirable to take part in the social and cultural activities of the community, though not at the cost of its normal functioning. Such participation will add to the goodwill towards the library. For the library staff members, such participations within limits give a break in their daily routine and increases social harmony.

REFERENCES

1. Narayana, G.J. Documentation services to an encyclopaedia. *International Review of Documentation* 31: 112-16, 1964.

12

Mentors : Inspiring Leaders

By and large, in everyone's career there is always the role of a mentor. The mentor may be a teacher, an immediate superior under whom one is working, a family member or someone in the profession whose contact develops into a bond that influences one's outlook on professional life, personal values and career path. In mentorship, there is a bond of emotionality that transcends to some extent the effects of status difference between the mentor and the other person in the relationship. In the case of inspiring leadership, the dominant influence is the inspiration drawn from the actions and behaviour of the leader in his or her interactions with the persons involved in the interaction. In the latter case, the personal relationship retains the effects of hierarchical difference between the leader and the members of the group. Given here are five such mentors and inspiring leaders who made a deep impact on me, and they are: Mr.N.M.Ketkar, Dr. S.R.Ranganathan, Prof. B. Anderson, Air Cdr. S.K Nair and Maj.Gen. Subba Rao. Not every 'leader' one comes across in one's career is necessarily good and inspiring, so included here is also the account of exceptions that I have experienced in my career.

1. MR. N. M. KETKAR

Mr. N.M. Ketkar was one of the most balanced personalities with deep concern for human values and scholarship I was fortunate to come across in my career. My first contact with him was at the Benaras Hindu University, Benaras (now Varansi) in 1954 where he was the Deputy Librarian, and I was a student of Library Science Course. His respect for all languages is seen when he expressed his desire to learn Kannada language from me, when he came to know that I am a Kannadiga. He left Benaras to take up the post of Chief Librarian at the Central Secretariat Library, Government of India at New Delhi, and later became the Director of the National Social Science Documentation Centre, Indian Council for Social Science Research, New Delhi. He played a key role in creating the opportunity for senior librarians from India to benefit from an educational tour of USA under the joint auspices of the Rockefeller Foundation and the Government of India. He was a mentor to me in the true sense of the term.(see also 2.1, 9.2 and 9.6)

Different Persons, Differing Images. It was a difficult situation for me to decide whether to accept or not the post of Scientist-C (library), in the Institute of Armament Studies (IAS) (later renamed as Institute of Armament Technology (IAT), and now Defence Institute of Armament Technology (DIAT) at Pune. To help me come out of the dilemma, I consulted three persons who could shed some light on the issue. Mr. N.M. Ketkar, who was from Pune and had some knowledge of IAS, advised me to take up the post. The reasons behind his advice were that IAS was a prestigious institute, it would provide ample opportunity to grow; and the work environment was good according to one of his relatives working in the institute at a senior level. Mr. Ratnam (name changed) had no knowledge about the institute, but had known one of the persons working in the Institute with whom I would have to deal with on a daily basis, if I joined there. He gave a scary picture of that person. He warned me to be extremely careful in dealing with that person, if I joined the Institute. When I asked him to elaborate his reservations with an example so that I could get an idea of what I should be careful about, his reply was: "you will know when you interact with him." The third person, Mr. Puri (name changed) was a civilian scientist who had worked at IAT for a year and recently returned to Delhi as he found the working environment there for civilian scientists quite horrid. When I requested him to explain further, he said that the Institute was totally dominated by the officers from the Army, the Navy and the Air force, and it was difficult for civilian scientists to cope with them.

The reality as experienced by me was that Mr. Ketkar was correct in his assessment, whereas Mr. Ratnam was very far from reality, and Mr.Puri was partially right. The fact was that IAT being an inter-services organization, officers from the three services and the civilian scientists worked together. Since the two sides were brought up in entirely different environments, it took time to understand each other. There was also the factor of social life in the campus which had a bearing on the assessment. IAT being a self contained campus, located far away from the city, where it was difficult to find suitable accommodation, most civilians coming from outside Pune opted to stay in the campus. The military side had its own well organized community institutions like the officer's mess, lady's club, sports club, and separate jawans' lungers where one could discern the existence of a system of hierarchy underneath. It became difficult initially for both civilian and service officers and their family members to adjust to this environment. It was a question of time and inclination to adjust to the military-civilian atmosphere. One distinctive advantage of serving in IAT was that the tenure of dean/directorship of the Institute was limited to about three years by rotation - the army, the navy, the air force and the civilian. Regarding the person (mentioned by Mr.Ratnam) with whom I was required to have constant dealing, I found him to be one of the most gentle, honest and dedicated colleague to work with.

Managerial insight : One's assessment of another agent-person, organization or situation is invariably shaped by the outcome of his or her encounters/interpersonal relationship with the other agent. There can be as many shades to the behavioural picture of the other agent as the number of persons viewing it. These differences in the perception are the result of genuine differences in the mode of perceiving, and value variation or the individual's biased/preconceived way of looking at things or a combination of them. One must weigh carefully the opinions of others while using it as an input in the decision making process and also in forming assessments of others.

2. DR.S.R.RANGANATHAN

His influence on the profession of librarianship in India and abroad, and his contributions to the field of librarianship are too well known. What is covered here is my experience. My personal contact with him was brief but most fruitful to me. It began in 1959, when I joined INSDOC, New Delhi.

Dr. Ranganathan, whenever he visited Delhi, used to stay with Shri. S. Parthasarathy, Head INSDOC, at the National Physical Laboratory (NPL) Staff Quarters in Pusa. His arrival would be known to his ex-students and other librarians interested in meeting him. When in Delhi, his morning routine included a long walk along the NPL road or in the campus of the Indian Agricultural Research Institute, Pusa. Those who wanted to benefit from his vast knowledge and practical experience would join him in the walk. He would select a topic and give a brief introduction of it, which included his line of thinking, and what was to be achieved. Then he would leave it open for discussion and further thinking. This is how the Research Group on the General Theory of Classification worked under his guidance on 'Common Property Isolates'.[1] If it was a project on bringing out a composite book, he would analyze the contents making up the book, assign to each participant her or his role/ task, and clarify doubts, if any. This is how the book "Documentation and its facets"[2] came to be written. The discussions were always focused. He never allowed his towering intellectual personality and high standing to come in the way of others' thinking or expressing what they thought. If the topic of study was research oriented, he would go deep into the problem and it was always very stimulating. He would give his reasons in case his thinking differed from the one expressed by others. There was no place for discussions on topics other than academic or professional. The walk would last for an hour and a half. It was sheer joy to learn under a great teacher in this manner. He had the gift of recognizing talent, inspiring even the ordinary and getting the best out of them.

One could say without hesitation that it was the golden era of Indian librarianship. The era produced a number of stalwarts like Shri. B .S. Kesavan of the National Library, Calcutta (later shifted to INSDOC, New Delhi), Prof. Dasguptha of Delhi University Library, Shri N. M. Ketkar of the Central Secretariat Library, New Delhi (later moved to ICSSR), Shri S.Parthasaratjhy of INSDOC, New Delhi, Pandit D. Subramanyam and Shri.G.R.Vishvanarthan of the Benaras Hindu University, Shri. Bashiruddin Ahemad of the Aligarh Muslim University, Prof. D. N.Marshall and Prof. B. Anderson of the University of Bombay, and Prof. K.S. Deshpande of Karnatak University, Dharwad. It is difficult to imagine the height to which the profession would have risen and the extent of benefits to the nation, if only the genius of Dr. Ranganathan and the extraordinary leadership of Shri. Kesavan had joined together.

Managerial insight : Dr. Ranganathan was a great teacher in the true tradition of "gurukula". There is no branch of library science and information science which has not benefited from his pioneering contributions. A unique feature of Ranganathan's personality was his deep knowledge of Indian culture, Hindu philosophy and mysticism, and deep mathematical background which he applied in the development of his theories on library science. It is not an exaggeration to call that period the 'Ranganathan Era'. He has left a number of admirers across the world and many disciples in India who worship him. He was a visionary who could see the link between library service and national development- social, cultural, educational, economic, industrial, scientific and technological. Sarada Ranganathan Endowment for Library Science established by him at Bengaluru is testimony to his selfless and complete dedication to the cause of librarianship.

3. PROF. B. ANDERSON

Prof. B.Anderson and Prof. D.N. Marsahall were the torch bearers of library profession in the old Bombay Province (comprising the present state of Maharashtra, parts of North Karnataka, and Gujarat). An entire generation of librarians in this part of the country owes their entry into the profession to them. Besides being pioneer librarians, they were also great teachers. The establishment of the library school in the University of Bombay is the result of their foresight. The starting of M.Lib.Sc. on the pattern of an open university, the first and the only University in the country to do so then is a testimony to their pragmatic and innovative approach to initiate advanced level library education. It is Prof. Anderson's mentorship that led to my entry into the field of library education. The following incident illustrates Prof. Anderson's great concern for the well being of his students.

I had enrolled for the Master's degree in Library Science in the University of Bombay in the year 1972. The course was of one year duration. The intake of students to the course was limited to an average of three to four students per year. This was mainly because there was no separate teaching staff recruited for the Course. Professor B. Anderson, the Librarian and Head, Department of Library Science and Prof. D. N Marshall, who had just retired as the Librarian of the University library, shared the classes between them.

The course was structured on the basis of self study and contact periods. The students had to attend classes for two months in two phases; the first phase at the beginning of the course and the second in the middle of the course. The classes were held daily during the two phases. Hence, I had to stay in Bombay to attend the classes. At that time I was employed at Pune in the Institute of Armament Technology. Though I stayed in Bombay, I was going to Pune for the weekend, leaving Bombay on Saturday evening after attending the two classes in the afternoon taken by Prof. Anderson and returning to Bombay on Monday morning. The first week went like this. The following Monday, Prof. Anderson announced in the class that he was reallocating the Saturday classes to Wednesday and Friday. I was quite happy about this shifting as this allowed me to leave Bombay on Friday evening. This enabled me to stay with my family for an additional day and also to attend to important work on Saturdays. Later, I came to know that Prof. Anderson shifted the Saturday classes to enable me to spend Saturdays too with my family. Taking additional classes on Fridays and Wednesdays were definitely a strain on him and also it dislocated his set schedule. He did not mind straining and inconveniencing himself if that benefited his student. It requires sensitivity of a rare order to feel tenderness towards others, putting aside one 's self interest and inconvenience. Another facet of his personality was his open-mindedness to scholarly issues which is reflected in the following incident. The dissertation part of the M.Lib.Sc. carried great weight in the assessment of the student's performance. My topic for the dissertation was *Management of ballistics information.* The first two chapters of the study were devoted to the history and development of ballistics, and the theory of ballistics respectively. Prof. Anderson felt that the first two chapters may be deleted as the topic of dissertation is library science and not ballistics. I expressed my strong desire to retain the two chapters as they provided the requisite foundation for the study. Next day he called me and approved the inclusion of the two chapters. Later, the project report was published as a monograph,[3] which was prescribed as a text book in two military schools because of its first two chapters.

Managerial insight : Concern for the well-being of students is an essential attribute of an outstanding teacher. Display of such concern goes a long way in creating a sense of respect and trust in the minds of students towards the teacher and the organization. The attribute of concern for the well-being of coworkers and subordinates also plays an important role in building harmonious relationship between the employer and the employee. Loyalty and trust are also factors that shape an individual's work behaviour. Openness of mind to others' viewpoints is another characteristic of real scholars and capable leaders.

4. AIR CDR. S.K. NAIR (AVSM)

He came to IAT as its Director and Dean in 1976. He is not a mentor in the sense that there was no apparent close personal relationship, but as a role model worthy of emulation— whether it is personal integrity, leadership qualities, managerial ability, work ethics or human values. His personality was such that his very presence created a dignified atmosphere that was conducive for openness of mind, feeling of sense of fairness from him, and the confidence in you that you get from him a clear, quick and right decision to a problem placed before him. Two instances are narrated here.

(a) Decision-making : Directors of Studies from the army, the navy and the air force wings of the Institute had been pressing for keeping open the library in the evening from 6 pm to night 10 pm., in addition to the normal working hours of 0730hrs to 1330 hrs. Their contention was that the service officers and student officers on courses did not find time during normal working hours to use the library. Since all of them live in the campus, keeping the library open in the night would enable them to make full use of it. Several times this issue was discussed in the Academic Council (AC) without arriving at a decision. I was not in favour of the proposal, principally for the reason that the premise that the students and staff members will use the library in the night was not valid; and there was the problem of arranging transport for the staff member assigned for the night duty, since all library staff stayed in the city, very far from the campus. The issue was raked up again in the AC meeting where the library was represented by the Chairman, Library Committee, when Air Cdr. Nair took charge as Director and Dean.

A day after the AC meeting, the library received an order asking to keep the library open from 6 pm to 10 pm. Following the order the library was kept open in the evening and night on a trial basis. A notable point was that Air Cdr. Nair was an active user of the library. When he visited the library later that day he asked me to maintain a separate register of attendance for the evening. During the two weeks that the library was kept open in the night, hardly any user visited the library, barring Air Cdr. Nair. One morning, after the completion of two weeks, the Director and Dean visited the library along with the three Directors of Studies. When we were in the classified documents section, where entry is restricted, he pronounced that there was no need to keep the library open for any extra time citing the attendance record. That was the end of the matter.

Managerial insight : To arrive at a right and effective managerial decision, the decision-maker has to take into consideration all relevant facts, and if necessary check the facts and their consequences. An outstanding decision-maker also chooses the correct time, place and mode to announce the decision. In the present instance, the Director avoided wasteful and possibly acrimonious discussion in the AC by choosing the appropriate time, place and the right persons to announce his decision.

(b) Leadership and vision : Most of the great leaders and change-makers in organizations are visionaries. It is an uncommon trait. Given here is one instance of visionary thinking of a great manager. The facts of the account given here are true, but it is not an exact replica of the format of the discussion that took place.

It was a morning in the late 1976. The place was IAT, Poona. The then Director and Dean was the late Air Cdre. S.K.Nair (AVSM). He had just returned after attending a short-term Computer Appreciation Course meant for very senior level defense personnel. The era was that of mainframe computers, whose installation occupied an entire room, and the country had only 4 or 5 computers. My telephone rings. I answer:

"Yes, Narayana speaking.

Sir, I am PA to Director speaking. The Director wants you to meet him now."

I meet him. The meeting was brief and to the point. It went as follows:

"Mr. Narayana, I have called you to discuss about using computers in the functioning of our library. Can't we try?

No Sir.

Why?

I had thought about it a year ago. That is, after I had completed a COBOL programming course conducted by ARDE Computer Centre. The main area where we could use computer is in cataloguing. We neither have a computer nor the Institute is likely to get one in the near future. Moreover, I found that catalogue processing by computer is not cost-effective.

You may be right, Mr. Narayana. But we must look beyond today. Computer holds the future, and we must prepare ourselves for facing that revolution from now itself... that day is not far off. It's true that we don't have a computer, but we can make use of the computer facility of the ARDE Computer Centre. In any new and innovative application of technology, cost factor, though important, becomes secondary. In all technological applications, unit cost begins decreasing with increasing production and time."

It took about three months for us in the library to successfully convert the first batch of our catalogue entries into e-format, with the wholehearted support of ARDE Computer Centre. It is to their credit that they specially designed the required software program that met all our requirements in such a short time. Thus, IAT Library and Information Centre (IC&L) became the first unit in the whole of DRDO, consisting of about 40 laboratories, establishments and field units, to introduce computer in library; and only the 2nd or 3rd library in the country. Further, it served as "best practice" for other units in DRDO to follow. By conferring on me the "Scientist of the Year Award - 1984" in the field of Information and Training, this contribution was recognized.

Managerial insight : The trait of perceiving vision is a hallmark of all great managers. A leader with vision inspires others working with him/her to give their best to the organization. Vision is a product of knowledge, rational forward thinking, perceiving, creativity and imagination about the future. Greatest obstacle to perceiving vision is one's mental block. Sometimes visions are born out of dreaming.

5. MAJ. GEN. N. SUBBA RAO (AVSM)

Making me aware of the educational function of libraries and the role of the librarian in it by Maj. Gen.Subba Rao has been stated in 8.1. Because of features that are inherent in a hierarchical organization structure and the existence of vast difference in level between the positions, there was no scope for building up of mentor relationship between us. For me, this shortage was made up by my learning from his managerial and leadership qualities. Things I learnt from him were— a) one need not be afraid of anybody in the organization including one's boss in any conflict, if he is right; b) honest and hard work brings its own reward, which will not remain unrecognized for ever; and c) decency requires following of established etiquette in vogue, without fail, as seen in the following episode.

My leaving IAT, Poona to join ADE, Bangalore has been

narrated earlier. This happened when Maj.Gen. Subba Rao was the Director and Dean of IAT. As per normal practice that on behalf of the organization the departing official is given a send off party.

Some how I was averse to have the send off party arranged for me and expressed this desire. This information reached the Director. He called me and strongly advised me not to be adamant about refusing to have the party. He told me the value of such gestures to the organization in enhancing its social asset and goodwill buildup, and for the individual its value as a record of service for later remembrances. Even after so many years, when ever I see the memento presented to me at the farewell party my memory goes back to my days at IAT, and cherishes those memories. I owe this to Maj. Gen. Subba Rao.

6. REVERSE MENTORING. DESIRE VS. ABILITY VS. ACTUALIZATION

Recently I wanted to revise my out of print book *Library and Information Management*[4] published in 1991. Since a lot of changes have taken place in the area of managing e-publications and digital technology part of libraries, with which my acquaintance and experience is dated, I wanted to associate one or two persons, having managerial experience in the area to join me as co-authors and to serve as reverse mentors. The essence of this new form of mentoring, started in industry, is the reversal of the role of mentor and mentee seen in the traditional pattern of mentoring. In the new paradigm, the mentor happens to be the young new generation members exposed to the current scientific and technological changes in a given field, and sharing their expertise, skills and experiences with the elderly/older members, i.e. mentors, in the organization.[5, 6] I could find two young and competent persons capable of doing justice to the task- one a lecturer in the School of Library and Information Science of a reputed university, and the other the librarian of a renowned Institute of Management. When I put the proposal before them, they were excited and were eager to join hands with me. We discussed in some detail the broad outline of the tasks involved and chapter-wise assignment of responsibility based on the expertise and experience of each of us. A tentative timetable was also arrived at. Each one of us was to first work out the broad sketch for the assigned chapters. It was agreed that the broad sketch/outline should be ready in 6 to 8 weeks, and the entire work to be completed in a year. Even after a few e-mail communications and telephone talks between us over a period of three months, things never started in right earnest. One of them could not find time to work as she had too many assignments on her hand; and the other had serious problems with her higher authorities, which was consuming all her time, energy and mental acumen, leaving little time to concentrate on writing for the book. I could understand their problems. Given this situation, I called off the project. I have no doubts on their competency and in their strong desire to join hands with me in accomplishing the task. But then, it would have been better for all three of us, had we balanced our desire against ability, and ability against action before arriving at the decision to cooperate.

Managerial insight : Dissonance between desire and ability, between ability and commitment, and between commitment and actualization is the biggest impediment that stands in the way of accomplishing a task or a project. When cooperation is voluntary, sometimes some persons find it difficult to say 'no' at the outset to a request for participation, probably due to their modesty or desire overtaking reality, though they know that they are unable to fulfill the commitment. It is better to say no at the outset, when one knows in advance one's limitations than later. In today's organizations latest technological expertise and skills is largely held by the new generation of young specialist workers. This has given rise to a new pattern of mentoring called reverse mentoring, where the young workers with expertise play the role of mentors.

7. A WATCHMAN CEO

The working hours of the ADE were 0730 hours to 1630 hours. A few employees of the establishment used to reach the exit gate 5 to 10 minutes before the closing time. However, the gate would open only after the 1630 hour siren. One day the Director had come to the gate to personally enforce discipline. A few workers who had gathered at the gate to go out were met by the security guards and were asked to meet the Director, who was standing some distance away from the gate. The Director scolded them and ordered them to go back to their respective work places and leave the work place only after the siren. On that particular day, I too had reached the gate some 5 minutes earlier as I had to meet someone in the Security section. The gatekeeper asked me to meet the Director, who was glaring at me from a distance. I did not meet him. As soon as the gate was opened, I made my exit. This incident became a talking point in the organization. The director earned the sobriquet "watchman director". I had expected that the Director would call me the next day to his office to take me to task over the issue, and charge me with indiscipline, but it never happened. An establishment which had amongst its top executives eminent leaders/managers also adorned a watchman CEO.

Managerial insight : There is nothing wrong in the Chief Executive of an organization insisting on employees to strictly adhere to the working hour norms. Instead of taking up the watchman's duty, he could have asked the administration to issue an order prohibiting staff members leaving their work places before time. A leadership move would have been to take up the issue in the Officers meeting or direct the heads of Divisions/ departments to ensure that employees under their charge strictly follow the timings. It is difficult to interpret the chief executive's behaviour on any rational basis. Probable causes could be any of the following: a) lack of confidence in the administration/ security apparatus; b) not sure of the correctness of his action; c) ego problem; and d) bureaucratic arrogance.

8. REFERENCES AND REFEREEING

References often play an important, and sometimes a decisive role in getting admission to reputed schools of learning, both in India and abroad; in the selection of candidates for award of scholarships/fellowships/internship; and in recruitment of persons for employment. References serve the purpose of providing background information on candidates as to their experience, knowledge, personality traits and abilities assessed by persons giving the letter of reference. Persons under whom an individual has worked for a reasonable period of time in an organization, and his or her mentors form the right persons to speak about the individual's abilities and personality traits. Hence, they constitute the most important source for references and refereeing.

There are firms which undertake background checks and also social professional networks which have specialized in conducting background checks (Business Standard, 2013).

Managerial insight : Value of a reference depends on the professional standing of the referee and his or her integrity. Usually, one names as referees his or her teacher, mentor or the person under whom one had worked and well acquainted with the ability and personality of the person to be reported upon. Now a days there are agencies which do the background check of a given person and provides the report.

REFERENCES

1. Ranganathan, S.R., Narayana, G.J. et al. Common Property Isolates. *Annals of Library Science* 7:1-12, 1960.
2. Ranganathan, S.R. Ed. Documentation and its Facets. Bombay, Asia Publishing, 1963.
3. Narayana, G.J. Ballistics : A Biblioview. Ballistics Information and Its Organization for Retrieval. Poona, Institution of Armament Technologists (India), 1977.
4. Narayana, G.J. Library and Information Management. New Delhi, Prentice-Hall of ndia, 1991.
5. Rekha Murali. Reverse mentoring. Hindu : Opportunities. Oct.31, 2012, p.1.
6. Kwoh, Leslie. Reverse Mentoring Cracks Workplace. The Wall Street Journal (India Edn.). Nov.28, 2011. (Wikiepedia).

13

Fulfilment

After serving the profession in varied capacities in different organizations for over 35 years, when I reminisce, there are several bits of experiences that have given me immense satisfaction, and the feeling that I have lived up to the expectations of the organizations where I served and of my superiors, barring some exceptions, with whom I was privileged to work with. The satisfaction derived from the recognition received from the users (see 7.4), the Scientist of the Year Award (see 11.4), and award of Fulbright Fellowship is already accounted. Apart from the sense of satisfaction derived from the recognition of one's achievements, creative contributions made towards the enrichment of the organization utilizing the given opportunities, there is another unique dimension to the feeling of fulfillment in professional life, which is born out of one's interpersonal relationships with others developed through her or his organizational roles. The following events, incidents and persons illustrate the part of interpersonal relationships in enriching that feeling of fulfillment in my professional life.

1. MRS. MERLYN'S (NAME CHANGED) GESTURE

It was my last working day at IAT. I was about to exit from my office. Mrs. Merlyn (name changed), my junior colleague, came to me with tears in her eyes, took my hand placed it on her head and asked me to bless her and her family. I sincerely prayed for her and her family members' well being. I assured her that god's blessings would always be with her. She being an orthodox Christian, her conduct of seeking my "asheerwad" deeply touched me. I could feel her sentiment, share her feelings, but what caused that mental frame in her was beyond my comprehension. I could think of such deep reverence reserved only to priests and religious gurus, and probably to great teachers. I have often wondered what service I did to her to deserve her deep regards towards me. She was posted to library on transfer from another department. She had no library qualification or library experience. The sudden transfer to an unfamiliar field of work had worked on her mind and she was quite apprehensive about her future career. I found her quite intelligent, willing to learn and capable of involving in work. Over the years she proved her worth in the library. On my part I tried to create opportunities for her to grow professionally and contribute to the good of the library, which she did admirably. I also tried to ensure successfully that her contributions to the organization were recognized and rewarded in terms of career promotions, and co-authorship. There is nothing extraordinary on my part in this. It was my duty as the senior member of the family to create a conducive and harmonious work environment in which each member played his or her part responsibly with dedication and hard work for the overall good of the organization. One thing that might have touched her consciousness might be that all through my service I had tried to maintain an open mind and fairness towards every person (including her) with whom I was associated irrespective of their social status, level of education, caste and community, region, gender, language and religion, i.e. tried to be honest and fair in dealing with them.

2. REMEMBRANCE OF A FORMER COLLEAGUE

One afternoon, Mrs. Leelavathi from ADE Knowledge Centre (KC) telephoned me telling that she was giving me some elating account involving me. What she narrated was something that deeply touched me. It was about the farewell party to Mr. M. Nadiger, Technical Officer working in the KC, given by the establishment on the occasion of his retirement from service. I had retired from ADE some twenty years before that event. Mrs. Leelavathi told me that even after a gap of so many years, Mr. Nadiger, while reminiscing his service in the organization, in his farewell speech, made a pointed reference to G.J.Narayana by expressing that whatever contributions he could make to the organization were the result of Mr. Narayana's initial guidance and inspiration drawn from him to strive for excellence in his work. Two other persons who had attended the function also narrated this to me.

His remembering of whatever little I had been able to impart to my colleagues in terms of shouldering higher responsibility, development of positive work culture, involvement, desire to achieve and creating a sense of duty towards users and the organization is an honour bestowed on me. So was the case with Mrs. Shanthamani of ADE Knowledge Centre remembering me on the eve of her retirement and Mrs. Leelavathi's regard for me. Words cannot express my feeling of fulfillment. I feel my indebtedness to him and a few others like him whose unstinted support helped me grow, who still remember me with warm regards and appreciation.

3. TRUE REWARDS OF TEACHING

As mentioned earlier, I had been teaching management science to the students of M.Lib.Sc. Course for nearly 15 years, right up to 1984. Nothing has given me as much satisfaction as teaching to this course and my interaction with the students. The highest reward for a teacher, according to me, is that the students really benefit from your teaching and interactions, grow up as leaders in their respective constituencies and become achievers. In this endeavor I have been fortunate. The sentiments expressed in the letter (extract reproduced) received by me, nearly twenty years after I gave up teaching, from one of my students strengthens my belief in what constitutes true rewards of teaching. The credit for this, to an equal measure, should go to the students.

"Today is Guru Purnima day and what better occasion than to reunite with you, my M.Lib. Course guru?. This Sunday when I started reading your introductory paras about how you had given the contents of the book as lectures to your M.Lib students etc, I had tears of nostalgia in my eyes, remembering the precious lectures with you, our discussions, your guidance etc. Scanning through the book and reading the important parts made me feel that you were standing in front of me and explaining all those topics. Just holding the book gave me some kind of moral support. I also felt proud that in my 27 year career at .... I have been able to sincerely practice good librarianship principles and contribute in a very significant way to all areas of work in the library, bringing efficiency to routine work, implementing innovative ideas. In 2008 when we were awarded the Technology Group award, it was thanks to my persistence that if as a team some of us have brought repute to the library by going beyond the line of duty to give services of a special kind to users, then we should be given credit for it. I made the statement of case and recommendations for nomination for the award, and it was indeed a proud moment to be conferred that award as a team! I have always felt that it is the blessings of persons like you and Riswadkar Sir that I have risen in my own stature.

Thank you, Sir for being a leading light both personally and professionally......".

Managerial insight : In Indian society, highest regard is reserved for teachers, doctors (considered as noble professions), priests and god men. However, genuine regards is shared only by teachers and doctors, since regard for priests and god men are born out of faith or fear. Even in the case of teachers and doctors the situation is changing rapidly due to increasing commercialization of the two professions overriding their service characteristic. Educational institutions have become factories preparing young men and young women for a job market. The concept of the development of the whole personality is increasingly jeered at. In other words, they have become a part of the service industry sector of the economy. A true teacher is one who not only imparts knowledge but also inspires students to absorb, appreciate, think, develop, and put into practice what is learnt from the teacher in their later careers. The relationship between a teacher and students is unique. On the part of the teacher, it is not sufficient that he is very well versed with the requisite knowledge that is to be transferred, but also has the ability to create trust in the teacher in the minds of students, and evoke right response in them. Besides these qualities, a true teacher goes beyond teaching what is prescribed in the curriculum, but also makes the students realize the importance of differentiating between knowledge and wisdom, permanent and transient values, good and bad management which will guide them to become successful managers and achievers in their respective fields of work. Out of the hundreds and thousands of students one has taught, it is only a few who reach that height. It is those few students who give the teacher the feeling of fulfillment in life, the highest reward a teacher can think of.

4. LECTURE AT THE "ADE LIBRARY DAY" FUNCTION

One morning Mrs. H.S.Leelavathi, my former colleague in ADE and at present the torchbearer of its Knowledge Centre telephoned to me stating that she and Dr.A.M.N.Yogi, Scientist F. and Head of Knowledge Centre (KC) were coming to my place in the evening. They wanted to invite me to deliver a lecture on a topic of my choice as a part of the "ADE Library Day" celebrations that was being organized. This gesture on the part of Mrs. Leelavathi and Dr. Yogi touched me deeply. There was no reason for her to think of me for the lecture. I had left ADE almost 25 years ago. When I asked them the reason behind my selection for the lecture, they mentioned that it was their way of honouring my valuable contributions to the development of the KC and the legacy I had left behind. The topic of my talk was "Successful Career: A Reflective Account". I was immensely pleased with the response from the audience to my talk. Later, I was told that the topic I had chosen was so appropriate and interesting that the authorities were thinking of inviting me to give another talk on the same topic for the benefit of the whole organization.

5. A GENUINE APPRECIATION OF MY BOOK

In the late1992, I was participating in a conference/ seminar organized by the Library, University of Poona. A co-participant met me and introduced herself as Mrs..., Professor of Library science in the Gujarat University. She said that she was keen to meet me I being the author of the book *Library and Information Management,* which was published in 1991. She told me that she was following my book in teaching library management to the students of M.Lib.Sc. What amazed me were her remarks that she could not believe that an Indian author could write such a fine book on library management. Until the publication of this book she had felt only American and British authors were capable of writing such standard books on the subject. I was immensely pleased to hear my book being commended. The satisfaction was because it came from a teacher teaching the subject and was unbiased as we had neither known each other earlier nor had any occasion arisen to get influenced about the merit of the book. It was nearly twenty years later that my attention was again drawn to the book by a publisher.

In 2012, a leading publisher from Delhi requested me to revise my book *Library and Information Management* published in 1991 by Prentice-Hall of India, New Delhi. He stated that he was writing to me after he happened to read through the book recently. The book was out of print for a long time. What surprised me was the publisher requesting me to revise the book, which meant that even after twenty years the book continues to be useful to those teaching and managing library and information centres. A search on the Internet showed that the syllabi of most universities in India have continued to prescribe this book to be referred by the students of B.Lib.Sc. and M.Lib.Sc.courses. One university had included this as a reference book even for M.Phil. students. More surprising (and satisfying my ego) was that as recent as 2010 three academicians (from Sri Lanka, Malaysia and New Delhi) had quoted passages from this book in their articles on information management. One leading information science research and teaching institution of international repute in India has framed their syllabus on information management part based on this book.

Managerial insight : Sometimes we do not know the value and worth of our contribution until someone competent in the field points it out. A work created keeping in mind a clearly defined purpose to be served and completed with best efforts never goes unrecognized.

6. A BOOK-SELLER'S TRIBUTE

Raka Book Agency, a leading book supplier in Pune was one of the approved suppliers of books to IAT. Mr. Desai, my colleague and I used to regularly visit his establishment to peruse the stock of recent publications received by them to select books of interest to IAT. Our relations with the firm always remained correct and cordial. No favours of whatever kind were expected or shown from either side. On our part, selection decisions were made and conveyed to the firm without delay and the bills were passed for payment within time. On their part, they had followed highest business ethics with us. I found nothing extraordinary about this library-supplier relationship until Prof. K.C.Sharma from the Faculty of Mathematics narrated to me about his visit to Mr. Raka in connection with buying a book, and the latter's remarks on me. Dr.Sharma told me that Mr. Raka revealed to him that in his long years of business, even though he has been supplying books to a large number of small and big libraries in Pune- academic, scientific research and business, he has never come across a librarian like Mr. Narayana, an epitome of high standard of ethics, efficiency in dealings and no tolerance for nonsense. "He is such a person that if I offer him a cup of tea as a normal courtesy, he would accept it only on the condition that he is allowed to pay for it", he said. This commendation coming from Mr. Raka, a leading book seller, a philanthropist and a person wedded to high ethical values was really heartening to me.

7. A PRINTER'S BENEVOLENCE TO SCHOLARLY PUBLISHING

I have mentioned earlier the publication of the book 'Ballistics: A Biblioview'. After my dissertation on ballistics information was accepted by the University of Bombay, I felt that it was appropriate that it should be made accessible to a wider section of users, particularly to those dealing with the subject of ballistics. Dr. K.C Sharma, Professor of Ballistics and Maj. H.S.N. Shastry of the Weapons Wing at IAT who had helped me with their expertise in writing the first two chapters of the report that dealt with the history and development of ballistics and the theory of ballistics, respectively concurred with my idea. They also felt that its publication as a monograph will be very useful as an introductory text to the students of ballistics. The problem was finding a suitable publisher. Since it would be a short monograph of interest to a limited but clearly defined set of users, the best way seemed to publish it myself. I had to find a printer.

My colleague and friend Mr. Desai took me to his friend Shri. V.V. Shingre, the owner of Sarvodaya Mudranalaya, Pune. We discussed and decided the format of the book, letter size, design, the cover page and the number of copies to be printed. When I asked him how much he would charge for printing, I was greatly touched to hear him say that he would get it printed free of cost. When I asked him why it was so, his gentle reply was, "you have put in so much time and efforts to write a scholarly work, let it be my humble contribution to the world of scholarship." The printing of the book was excellent.

The book received an excellent review in 'The National Defense', the foremost international journal on defence matters published from America. Air Cdr. S.K Nair, the Dean of IAT commended the book by writing, "Besides being of direct interest to practising librarians, the book should be of use to ballistics research workers and armament designers as it gives a valuable and neatly consolidated overview of published literature."

8. IN THE PRESENCE OF MRS. INDIRA GANDHI, THE HON. EX-PRIME MINISTER OF INDIA

It is a rare and astounding experience for anyone to stand before Mrs. Indira Gandhi, the late Hon. Prime Minister of India, who could dare Mr. Richard Nixon, the then President of America, the foremost super power at the time. This event came to me in the form of receiving the Scientist of the Year Award-1983 from her on 13th January 1984. The award and the medal was bestowed on me in recognition of my contributions to the Defence Research and Development Organization, Ministry of Defence, Government of India in the area of information and training, while managing the Information Centre and Library of the Institute of Armament Technology, Poona. It was also a unique honour to be a part of the dinner party arranged in her honour after the presentation ceremony.

When I think back of this momentous event that occurred in my career nearly 35 years ego, what remains in my memory now is the picture of me standing before a frail lady, but so powerful and charismatic a personality that my mind went blank for a few seconds.

Managerial insight : This account is beyond analysis. At the most, it can be said that complete devotion to one's profession, honest and creative discharge of one's duties is bound to get its just reward, but not as a rule.

CLOSURE

People constituting a society fall into three categories: nobody, anybody and somebody. To become somebody, one must be bestowed with or develop the traits of keen observation, a questioning mind, ability to take reasonable risks and complete involvement in the chosen task, project or enterprise. I have strived all through my professional life to become somebody, rather than nobody or anybody. This has given me the sense of fulfillment. Following this path has not been easy as I had to trade off, on many occasions, my personal interest for organizational interest, and the interests of persons working with me. It will not be an exaggeration to say that to a large extent, it is the influence of my mentors, the contributions of my co-workers and exploiting the opportunities that were there, but were not apparent, that has helped me to become somebody. It has not been an easy course to tread. It also requires a certain amount of luck. In following this path I have met with both roses and thorns, roses outnumbering the thorns.

Index